PowerPoint 2000
Creating and using slide shows

Copyright - Editions ENI - May 2000
ISBN: 2-7460-0975-7
Original edition: 2-7460-0715-0

ENI Publishing LTD

500 Chiswick High Road
London W4 5RG

Tel: 020 8956 2320
Fax: 020 8956 2321

e-mail: publishing@ediENI.com
http://www.publishing-eni.com

Editions ENI

BP 32125
44021 NANTES Cedex 1

Tel: (33) 02.51.80.15.15
Fax: (33) 02.51.80.15.16

e-mail: editions@ediENI.com
http://www.editions-eni.com

Finding Your Way collection directed by Corinne HERVO
Translated from the French by Elisabeth BLAMIRE

FOREWORD

The **Finding Your Way** collection is aimed at people with no previous experience in computing. It has been put together to give you clear and detailed explanations, using precise and simple terms. These explanations keep to the rule "one description, one illustration": each command is illustrated with a dialog box or a screen showing an example:

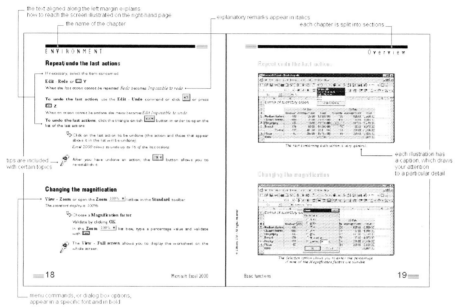

To give you as wide an introduction to the software as possible, all the methods of performing each task have been described. The following icons have been used to identify them: (menu method), (mouse method) and (keyboard method).

Every book in the **Finding Your Way** collection is organised in chapters, which are split into sections dealing with particular topics. The general layout of the book is presented in the **Table of contents**, which you will find on the following pages.

The book includes an appendix with a list of the shortcut keys available and an **Index**, for finding information quickly.

CONTENTS

CREATING OBJECTS　　　　　　　　**Chapter 6**

■ TABLES

■ PICTURES

■ SOUNDS/VIDEOS

■ DRAWINGS

■ **MANAGING OBJECTS**

■ **FORMATTING OBJECTS**

APPENDICES

Chapter **1**

POWERPOINT 2000

Starting PowerPoint 2000

Click the **Start** button on the taskbar at the bottom of the screen then drag the mouse pointer to the **Programs** option.

The contents of the Programs menu appear on screen.

Click the **Microsoft PowerPoint** option.

A dialog box asks if you want to create a new presentation or open an existing presentation.

 You can **Create a new presentation** using:

- the **AutoContent Wizard** which allows you to define the organisation of a presentation with the help of a predefined template.
- the **Design Template** option allows you to choose a presentation template.
- the **Blank presentation** option will open a new presentation.

or you can **Open an existing presentation** by selecting one of the last presentations opened from the list shown.

Confirm your choice by clicking **OK**.

If you have chosen to create a new presentation, the New Slide dialog box appears.

 Depending on the dialog box that appears, answer the questions you are asked. In the **New Slide** dialog box, choose one of the page layouts and click **OK**.

The workscreen appears.

Microsoft
PowerPoint

 This icon might appear on the Windows desktop: . If this is the case, double-click this icon to start PowerPoint.

Starting PowerPoint 2000

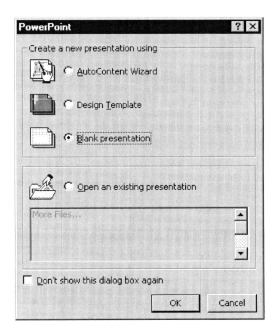

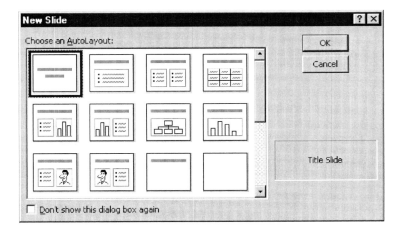

Creating and using slide shows

Discovering the application window

The workscreen appears when you start PowerPoint.

> **The title bar and icons (a)**: to the left, PowerPoint's **Control** menu icon ⌨, followed by the name of the application (**Microsoft Power-Point**) and the name of the active document.
> To the right, the **Minimize** button ⬕ allows you to minimise the window without closing the application; the **Restore** button ⬘ reduces the size of the window so that it no longer takes up the whole screen; in this case the **Restore** button gives way to the **Maximize** button ⬜, which restores the window to the full screen; finally, the **Close** button ⬗ allows you to leave the application.
>
> **The menu bar (b)** contains all the PowerPoint menus including a help menu. Each menu includes a list of the commands available as you work.
>
> **The Standard** and **Formatting toolbars (c)**: these tools allow you to carry out certain commands quickly, such as saving a presentation. If these bars are not visible on the screen, you can activate the **Standard** and **Formatting** options in the **View - Toolbars** menu.
>
> **The Drawing toolbar (d)** allows you to draw, manage and present objects. If this bar is not visible on the screen, you can activate the **Drawing** option in the **Views - Toolbars** menu.
>
> **The Status bar (e)**: this bar shows the number of the current slide, the total number of slides in the presentation and the name of the template in use. If you want to show or hide this bar, use **Tools - Options**, and in the **View** tab, activate or deactivate the **Status bar** option.

When you start PowerPoint 2000, the **Standard** and **Formatting** toolbars are shown on the same line.

Discovering the application window

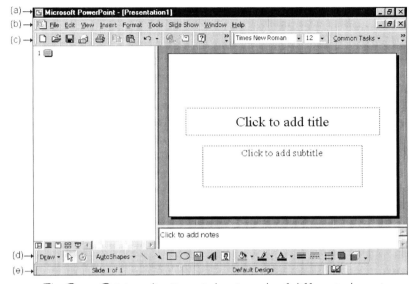

The PowerPoint application window is made of different elements.

Discovering the presentation window

The title bar (a): to the left, the presentation's **Control** menu 🔲 followed by the name of the active presentation. To the right, the **Minimize** (🔳), **Maximize** 🔲 or **Restore** 🔳 buttons allow you to manage the size of the window; finally, the **Close** button ☒ closes the presentation.

The workspace (b): this is the area in which you create slides. Its appearance depends on the current view.

The view buttons (c): these tools allow you to activate the best view for the work you are currently doing.

The scroll bars (d) and the **scroll cursors (e)** can be used to move around the length and breadth of the window.

Using the menus on the menu bar

To open a menu, point to the name of the menu and click with the mouse or hold down the ⌗Alt⌗ key and type the letter that is underlined in the menu's name.

⬗ When you open a menu, the standard options appear by default. If you want to see a complete list of the menu options, click ⬙, wait for 5 seconds or double-click the menu's name.

The options that appear grey are currently unavailable: commands that are followed by an ellipsis open a dialog box. Black triangles signal the presence of sub-menus.

To close a menu, point and click elsewhere on the screen, press ⌗Esc⌗ twice or press ⌗Alt⌗ .

To run a command, point to the relevant option and click, or type the letter that is underlined in the option without pressing ⌗Enter⌗ .

 The contents of PowerPoint 2000 menus change according to the commands you used most recently.

Discovering the presentation window

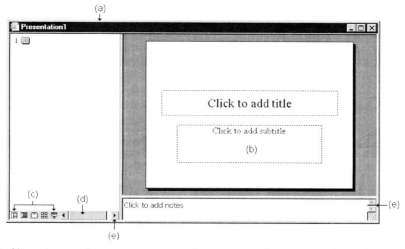

In Normal view, the presentation window contains three panes: the outline pane to the left, the slide pane, and the notes pane at the bottom on the right.

Using the menus on the menu bar

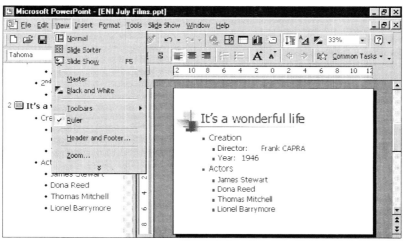

When an icon appears to the left of an option, clicking this icon on one of the toolbars can also run the command.

Using the Office Assistant

When you need advice, ask the Office Assistant.

To show the Office Assistant, open the **Help** menu and activate the **Show the Office Assistant** command. To ask for help with the current task, click the Office Assistant.

> To see the help about one of the proposed points, click that point. If your query does not concern one of these points, enter a question and click the **Search** button and select the topic you are interested in.
>
> *The corresponding help menu appears.*
>
> Consult the help.
>
> Click the ☒ button to close the window.

Changing the appearance of the Office Assistant

Click the Office Assistant then click the **Options** button.

If a dialog box is open, the Options button is not available. If this is the case, close the dialog box by clicking ☒ then start again.

Click the **Gallery** tab.

> Click the **Back** and/or **Next** buttons to find the Assistant you want.
>
> When you have chosen your Assistant, click **OK**.
>
> If prompted, insert the Microsoft Office 2000 CD into your CD-ROM drive then click **OK** again to confirm the change of Assistant.

 When a light bulb appears in a slide, the Assistant has a tip for you. Click the light bulb to see the tip.

Using the Office Assistant

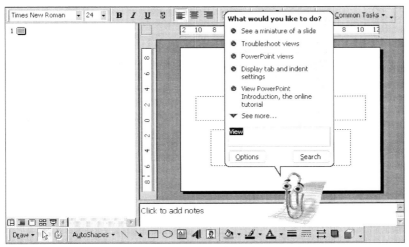

*A window appears with a list of topics about
your current task or the question you typed.*

Changing the appearance of the Office Assistant

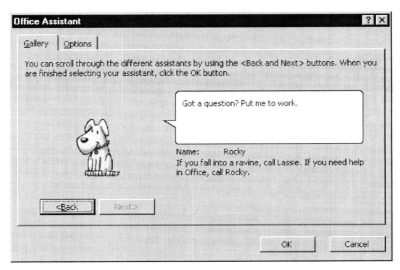

There are eight Office Assistants.

Creating and using slide shows

Consulting help at Microsoft's site

When the PowerPoint help cannot answer your question, you can look for help on Microsoft's site.

Help - Office on the Web

The browser window opens at Microsoft's site. You can now look at Microsoft's help.

Search for help.

> When you have finished, close the browser window by clicking ⊠.

Undoing your actions

To undo the last action, use **Edit - Undo**, click the ↺ tool button or press `Ctrl` **Z**. *When PowerPoint cannot undo an action, **Can't Undo** appears in the **Edit** menu.*

To undo the last actions, open the list of recent actions by clicking the downwards arrow on the ↺▾ tool button.

> Click the last action you want to undo (this action and all those that followed it will be undone).
>
> *Unless you change this setting, you can undo up to 20 of your last actions.*

 To redo an action you have undone, use the ↻▾ tool button.

Consulting help at Microsoft's site

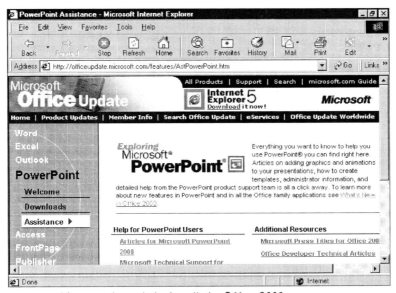

You can obtain help for all the Office 2000 programs.

Undoing your actions

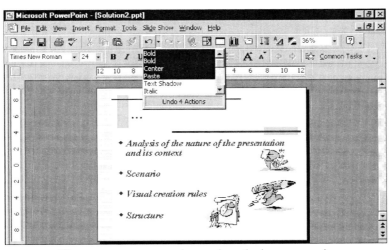

The actions you can undo are described very vaguely.

Creating and using slide shows

Repeating the last action

Rather than doing the same task several times, you can repeat your last action.

Edit - Repeat or Ctrl **Y** or F4

 If no action can be repeated, the **Edit** menu contains **Can't Repeat.**

Leaving PowerPoint 2000

Once you have finished working in PowerPoint, you can leave PowerPoint and close the application window.

File - Exit or click the X button on the application window, or press Alt F4 .

If you try to close PowerPoint without having saved a presentation that you have edited, a warning message appears.

 To save the presentation, click **Yes.**

If your document has never been saved before PowerPoint suggests you give it a name.

To leave PowerPoint without saving the presentation, click **No.**

To stay in PowerPoint, click **Cancel.**

Repeating the last action

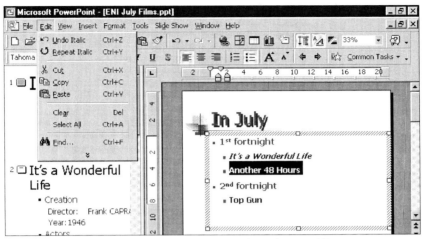

*The name of the action appears after the word **Repeat**.*

Leaving PowerPoint 2000

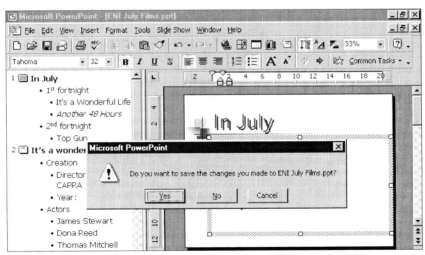

*This alert message appears when you close PowerPoint without
having saved a presentation.*

Creating and using slide shows

Changing the view

PowerPoint offers several views, and you can choose which one best suits the work you are currently doing.

To work with one slide in Normal view, use the **View - Normal** command, or click the ⬚ button in the bottom left of the presentation window. The ⬚F6⬚ key allows you to move from one pane to another.

To work on one slide in Slide view, click ⬚.

✍ **To see all the slides in the presentation as miniatures**, use **View - Slide Sorter** or click the ⬚ tool in the bottom left of the presentation window.

✍ **To increase the size of the outline** pane for all the slides in the presentation, click the ⬚ button in the bottom left of the presentation window.

This view allows you to organise the slides quickly.

To show a slide with a notes page, use **View - Notes Page**.

This view allows you to enter and edit comments about the slide.

 To go from **Slide Sorter** view to a view of an individual slide, you can double-click the slide you want to see.

Changing the view

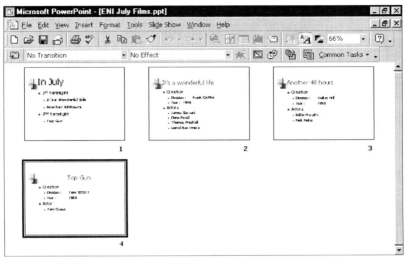

This view activates the Slide Sorter toolbar.

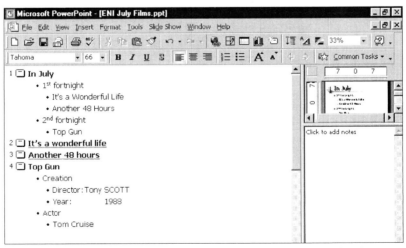

You can change the size of each pane by dragging its grey border.

Creating and using slide shows

Scrolling through the slides in Normal and Slide view

To go to the previous slide, click ▲ or press `Pg Up`.

To go to the next slide, click ▼ or press `Pg Dn`.

To go to a particular slide, drag the scroll cursor up or down the vertical scroll bar.

The number of the slide followed by the total number of slides in the presentation, and the title of the slide are shown in a ScreenTip.

When the name and number of the slide you want appear in the ScreenTip, release the mouse.

 You can also reach the first slide by pressing `Ctrl` `Home` and the last with `End`, as long as you are not in a text box.

Changing the zoom

The zoom can be used to display your document in large format or to obtain a more general, smaller view.

Open the **Zoom** list box `26%` ▼ on the **Standard** toolbar by clicking the black triangle.

The default zoom value depends on your screen, the current view and the toolbars that are shown, and your screen resolution. The percentages in the list depend on the current view.

Choose one of the zoom percentages by clicking the one you want, or you can enter a precise value and confirm by pressing `Enter`.

 You can also access different zoom values via **View - Zoom**.

Scrolling through the slides in Normal and Slide view

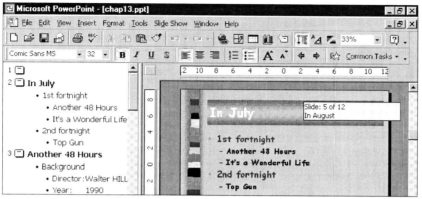

In this example, slide 5, with the title In August, is going to be shown.
There are 12 slides in the presentation.

Changing the zoom

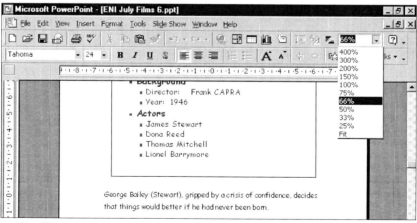

The **Fit** option, available in the Slide pane, leaves PowerPoint to calculate
the zoom so that the whole slide fits on the screen.

Creating and using slide shows

Showing/hiding the rulers

The rulers cannot be shown in Slide Sorter view.

> **To show the rulers**, use the **View - Ruler** command.

*A tick appears to the left of the **Ruler** option.*

To hide the rulers, use the **View - Ruler** command again.

*If the vertical ruler does not appear, use **Tools - Options**, click the **View** tab, and activate the **Vertical ruler** option.*

Discovering the snap feature

When the snap feature is active, objects appear to be attracted to a grid or shape.

To choose which snap feature you want to use, click the **Draw** button on the **Drawing** toolbar and point to the **Snap** option.

> Depending on the snap feature you want, activate or deactivate the following options:

To Grid	if this choice is active, when you drag or draw an object or shape, it aligns itself on the intersection of the closest lines of an invisible grid.
To Shape	if this choice is active, objects are automatically aligned to gridlines that pass along the vertical and horizontal borders of other objects in the presentation.

To drag objects freely, press the ⌗Alt⌗ key while you drag.

Showing/hiding the rulers

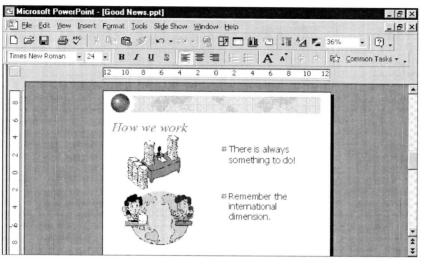

Two rulers graduated in centimetres (or in inches, depending on your configuration) appear: one vertical, one horizontal.

Discovering the snap feature

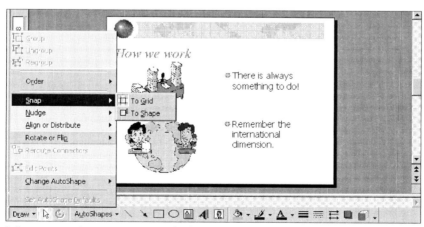

When a snap feature is active, the button to the left of the option is pressed in.

Creating and using slide shows

Using the guides

You can only use the guides when you are in Normal, Slide or Notes Page view.

To show/hide the guides, use **View - Guides**.

A horizontal and a vertical guide appear, crossing in the middle of the slide.

To move a guide, you need to show them first.

 Click the guide you want to move then drag it.

As you drag, PowerPoint displays the distance that separates the guide from the central point.

Release the mouse once you have dragged the guide as far as you want.

The higher the zoom you choose, the more precisely you can move the guides.

Managing the toolbars

To float a toolbar, point to the vertical line at the left of a docked toolbar and drag it into the workspace.

To dock a toolbar without choosing its location, double-click its title.

To dock a toolbar and choose its location, point to its title bar and drag it to its new position.

Release the mouse once you reach the bar's new location.

To see all the buttons on a toolbar, click the 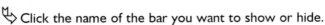 button.

To hide or show a toolbar, use the **View - Toolbars** command, or right-click one of the bars you can see.

 Click the name of the bar you want to show or hide.

 When all the bars are hidden, use **View - Toolbars** to open them again.

Using the guides

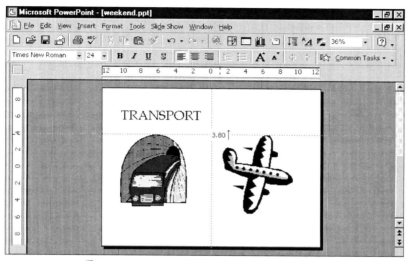

The guides appear on the slide as dotted lines.

Managing the toolbars

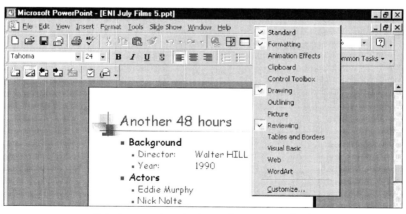

A tick precedes the bars that are on display.

Creating and using slide shows

Selecting one or more objects

To select one text type object, click the text concerned, if necessary, and point to the frame that represents the text object. When the pointer takes the shape of a four-headed arrow, click or press `Esc`.

To select any other type of object, click in the object if it has a fill, or click one of its borders if it does not.

> **To select several objects**, select the first object, and then `⇧ Shift`-click the following objects, or click the `◄` tool button and drag around the objects to select them.
>
> **To select all the objects**, use **Edit - Select All** or press `Ctrl` **A**.

Selecting slides

Go to **Slide Sorter** view: **View - Slide Sorter** or click the `▦` button in the bottom left of the presentation window.

Click the first slide you want to select.

> Press `Ctrl` and click each slide you want to select, without releasing the `Ctrl` key.
>
> *You can also drag around the slides you want to select.*

 If you have selected a slide by mistake, remove it from the selection by `Ctrl`-clicking it again.

Selecting one or more objects

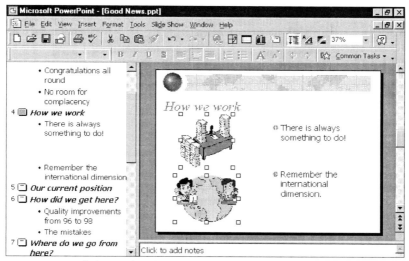

Selection handles surround each selected object.

Selecting slides

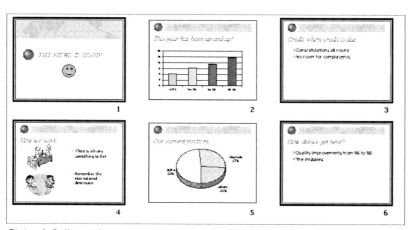

Slides 1, 3, 4 and 6 are selected here: the borders of these slides are thicker.

Moving/copying a slide using the clipboard

Go to **Normal** view: **View - Normal** or click the ⊞ button in the bottom left of the presentation window.

Select the slide you want to move or copy by clicking its icon in the Outline pane.

To move the slides, use **Edit - Cut** or ✂ or ⌨Ctrl **X**.

To copy the slides, use **Edit - Copy** or ▤ or ⌨Ctrl **C**.

If you are moving the slides, the selection disappears and is placed on the clipboard. If you are copying the slides, the selection is copied onto the clipboard.

Select the slide after which you want to place the selection.

Edit - Paste or ▤ or ⌨Ctrl **V**

The contents of the clipboard are placed after the active slide.

 Go to Slide Sorter view if you want to move/copy several slides.

Moving/copying a slide with the mouse

Go to **Slide Sorter** view: **View - Slide Sorter** or click the ⊞ button in the bottom left of the presentation window.

Select the slides you want to move or copy.

Point to one of the selected slides.

If you are moving the slides, drag the selection to its new position.

If you are copying the slides, press ⌨Ctrl and drag the selection to the destination of the copy.

As you move the slides, the mouse pointer is accompanied by a rectangle, and as you copy the slides, the pointer is accompanied by a plus sign.

 To move a slide in Normal or Outline view, drag its icon.

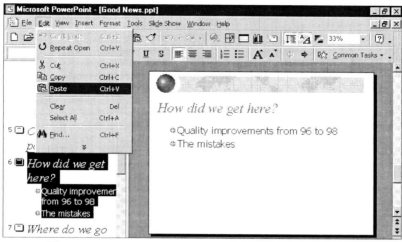

The contents of the clipboard will be inserted after slide 6.

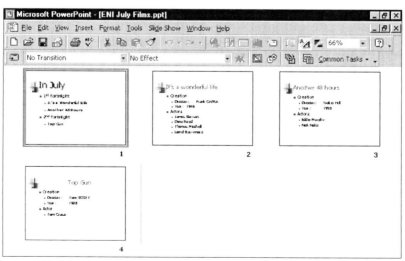

Slide 1 will be moved to the position of the vertical line.

Creating and using slide shows

Moving/copying an object inside a slide

Select the object you want to move or copy (which might be a picture, text, or a title, for example).

Point to the selection and make sure that the mouse pointer becomes a four-headed arrow.

> **If you want to move the selection**, drag it to its new position and release the mouse button.
>
> **If you want to copy the selection**, hold down the `Ctrl` key as you drag the selection.
>
> *A plus sign accompanies the mouse pointer.*
>
> Release the `Ctrl` key then the mouse button.
>
> *You can duplicate an object by selecting it then using **Edit - Duplicate** (or `Ctrl` **D**). The duplicate is slightly offset in relation to the original.*

Moving/copying an object from one slide to another

Select the object you want to copy or move.

If you want to move the selection, use Edit - Cut or ✂ or `Ctrl` **X**.

If you want to copy the selection, use Edit - Copy or 📋 or `Ctrl` **C**.

If you are moving the selection, it disappears and is placed on the clipboard. If you are copying the selection, it is copied onto the clipboard.

Go to the destination slide using the ▲ and ▼ buttons on the vertical scroll bar.

> Edit - Paste or 📋 or `Ctrl` **V**

Moving/copying an object inside a slide

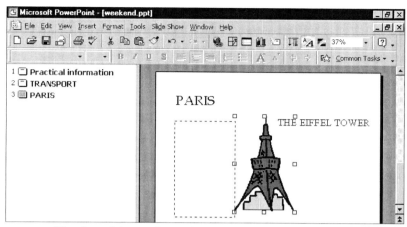

The dotted frame shows the future position of the object.

Moving/copying an object from one slide to another

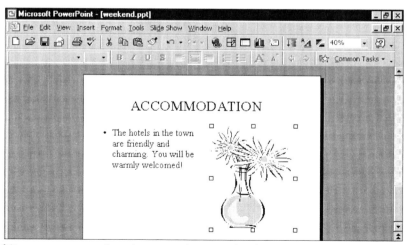

After you paste it, the selection is shown with selection handles. You can paste it several times in a row, because it remains on the clipboard.

Creating and using slide shows

Using the Clipboard toolbar

If you need to, show the **Clipboard** toolbar using **View - Toolbars - Clipboard**.

The Clipboard toolbar opens automatically after the second consecutive copy.

Select the objects concerned and transfer them to the clipboard using **Copy** or **Cut**. Do this as many times as is necessary.

> ✋ Activate the destination slide.

> *The selected objects are shown as icons on the **Clipboard** toolbar.*

> To paste a selection from the **Clipboard** toolbar, click the corresponding icon.

> To paste all the selections shown, click the [🗒 Paste All] button.

> Close the **Clipboard** toolbar by clicking the [✕] button or by deactivating the **Clipboard** option in the **View - Toolbars** menu.

> 🔑 Empty the clipboard by clicking [🖾] on the **Clipboard** toolbar, or by closing all your Microsoft Office applications.

Copying text/object formatting

Select the text or object whose formatting you want to copy.

If you only want to make one copy, click the tool button on the **Standard** toolbar, and to make several copies, double-click this tool.

If necessary, go to the slide that contains the text or the object concerned by the copy using the [⬆] and [⬇] buttons.

> ✋ Select the text or object concerned by the copy.

> If you have double-clicked the format painter tool, leave the copying process by pressing [Esc], or click the [🖌] tool button on the **Standard** toolbar again.

Using the Clipboard toolbar

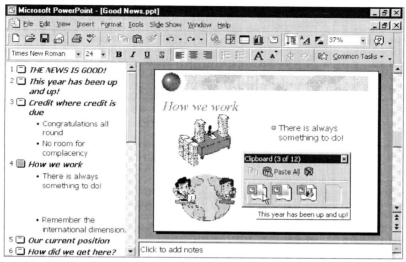

If you point to an icon (without clicking), a ScreenTip shows the first characters in the copied object, or its number if it is a picture.

Copying text/object formatting

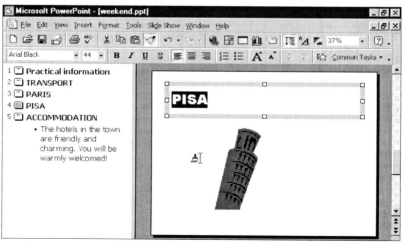

In the workspace, the mouse pointer takes the shape of a paintbrush.

Changing the slide page setup

File - Page Setup

In the **Slides sized for** list, choose the option **On-screen show, Letter Paper, A4 Paper, 35 mm Slides, Overhead, Banner** or **Custom**.

PowerPoint adapts the Width and Height values to the format you have selected.

In the **Slides** frame, choose the printing orientation of the slides. Click the **Portrait** option for the slides to have a vertical orientation, or **Landscape** if they are to have a horizontal orientation.

In the **Notes, handouts & outline** frame choose the printing orientation you want for notes pages, handouts and outlines.

Click **OK** to confirm your choices.

Changing the slide page setup

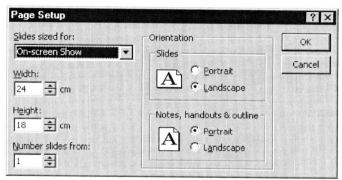

*By default, the slide format is **On-screen Show** with a **Width** of 24 cm and a **Height** of 18 cm.*

Printing a presentation

Select the slides you want to print. If you want to print all the slides in a presentation, you do not have to make any selections.

File - Print or Ctrl **P**

✎ In the **Print range** frame, define which slides you want to print:

All	to print all the slides in the presentation.
Current slide	to print the slide where the insertion point is.
Selection	to print the slides you have previously selected.
Slides	to print the slides you enter in the following text box. Type the numbers of the slides, separated by a comma if they are not consecutive, or with a hyphen if they are.

In the **Copies** frame, enter the **Number of copies** you want to print.

Open the **Print what** drop-down list and choose what you want to print: **Slides**, **Handouts** (to print several slides per page), **Notes Pages** or **Outline View** (the contents of the outline pane).

If you have chosen the **Handouts** option, indicate the number of slides to be printed on each page in the **Handouts** frame.

If you are printing on a black and white printer, activate:

Grayscale	to optimise the appearance of colour slides.
Pure black and white	to print the whole presentation in black and white by transforming the shades of grey into black and white.

Activate the **Scale to fit paper** option if you want to increase or decrease the image of the slides so that they fill the whole printed page. Depending on your requirements, choose whether or not to **Frame slides**.

Start printing by clicking **OK**.

 The 🖨 tool button on the **Standard** toolbar prints the presentation without passing by the dialog box.

Printing a presentation

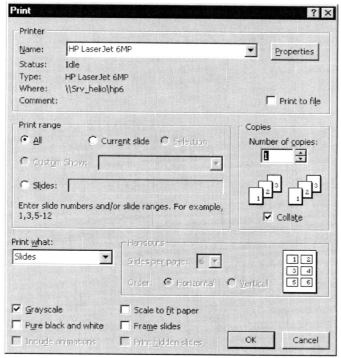

*If you are printing several copies, activate the **Collate** option
to tell PowerPoint to print one complete copy
before starting the next one.*

PERSONAL NOTES

Chapter 2

PRESENTATIONS

41

Opening a presentation

If you want to edit a presentation that has already been saved, you need to open it to see it on screen.

File - Open or 🗁 or Ctrl **O**

 ↳ Choose the disk drive that contains the presentation you want to open by clicking the black triangle at the right of the **Look in** text box.

*The **My Documents** folder is selected in the **Look in** list by default. This list contains all the drives you can access on your computer (the floppy disk drive (A:), the hard disk (C:), and possibly a CD-ROM drive). There may also be a network (**Network Neighborhood**).*

Go to the folder that contains the presentation you want to open by double-clicking the folder's yellow icon.

*The folder's name is now shown in the **Look in** box.*

To go to the parent folder, click the ⬆ button.

 ↳ To see a detailed list, open the list on the ▦ tool and choose **Details**.

To see the properties of a presentation, click the name of the presentation in question, open the list on the ▦ tool and click the **Properties** option.

To see a preview of the contents of a presentation, click the presentation's name, open the ▦ list and click **Preview**.

The first slide in the presentation appears in the right of the dialog box.

Return to the standard list by opening the ▦ list and choosing **List**.

Open a presentation by double-clicking its name or by selecting it then clicking **Open**. If you want to open several presentations, use the ⇧ Shift and Ctrl keys to select them before clicking **Open**.

 If you want to open one of the last four presentations you worked on, open the **File** menu then click the name of the presentation in question.

Opening a presentation

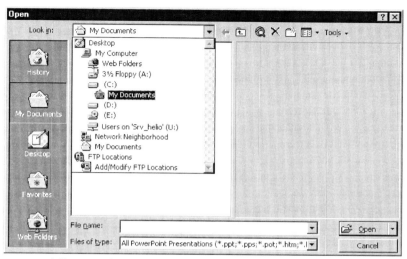

When you drag the mouse (without clicking) over the icons
in the dialog box, their names are shown.

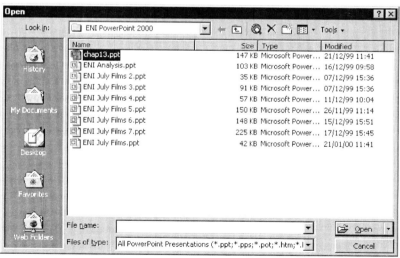

In this example you can see a detailed list of the presentations
in the *ENI PowerPoint 2000* folder.

Closing a presentation

When you have finished working on a presentation you can close it.

File - Close or click the ⊠ button in the document window, or even press `Ctrl` `F4`

When no presentations are open, only the application window is visible.

> ↳ If you have not saved the last changes, click:
>
> | **Yes** | to save the presentation before closing it. |
> | **No** | to close the presentation without saving the changes. |
> | **Cancel** | to leave the presentation open. |

Saving a new presentation

If you want to use a presentation again, you need to save it on your hard drive.

File - Save or 💾 or `Ctrl` **S**

The Save As dialog box appears, and the default location for your presentation is the My Documents folder.

Type the name you want to give to your presentation in the **File name** box.

Open the **Save in** drop-down list by clicking the black triangle in the right of the text box and choose the drive where you want to save your presentation.

> ↳ Double-click the name of the folder in which you want to save the presentation.
>
> *The name of the folder appears in the Save in box.*
>
> Click the **Save** button.
>
> *The name of the presentation, possibly followed by its extension, appears on the title bar. A PowerPoint document has the extension .PPT, although the extension does not necessarily appear.*

 The **File - Save As** command can be used to save an existing presentation under a different name.

Closing a presentation

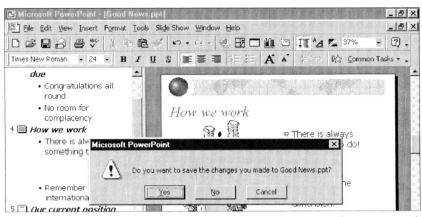

This message appears when you try to close a presentation you have not saved.

Saving a new presentation

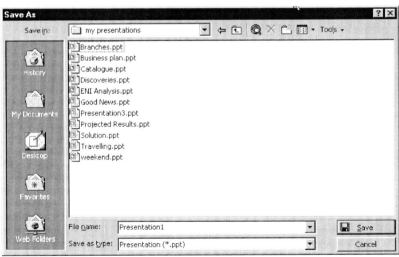

A document name can contain up to 255 characters, including spaces.

Saving an existing presentation

If you have made changes to an existing presentation, you might want to keep the changes you have made, so you will need to save them.

File - Save or 🖫 or ⌨Ctrl **S**

The Save As dialog box does not appear because you have already saved the presentation and given it a name. Only the changes you have made are saved.

Creating a new presentation

File - New

The New Presentation dialog box offers different templates that can be used, grouped under three tabs.

       ☞ Click the tab that contains the template you want to use.

       The Presentations tab contains the AutoContent Wizard templates.

       Select the name of the template and click the **OK** button, or simply double-click the name of the template.

       Select the layout for the first slide and click **OK**.

       The 🗋 tool or the ⌨Ctrl **N** shortcut key combination can be used to create a new presentation based on the **Blank Presentation** template.

Saving an existing presentation

*The changes made to the **weekend** presentation will be saved.*

Creating a new presentation

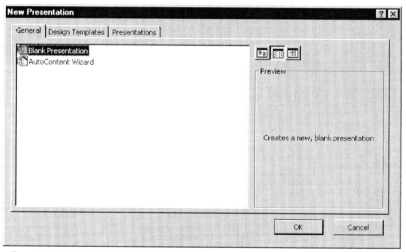

*The **Blank Presentation** template allows you to create a blank presentation using the default template.*

Creating and using slide shows

Packing a presentation

If you want to transfer a presentation from one computer to another, you can compress it.

If necessary, save the presentation(s) you want to compress.
File - Pack and Go
A wizard will guide you through the process.

If the Office Assistant appears, tell him **No, don't provide help now**, and then click the **Next** button in the wizard window.
Indicate which presentation you want to pack: the **Active presentation** or **Other presentation(s)**.
Click **Next**.

> Choose the destination of the compressed file: a floppy disk or perhaps another computer. If you choose to a floppy disk, insert it in the appropriate drive.
> Click **Next**.
> Indicate whether you want to **Include linked files** (sounds, videos, presentations) or **Embed True Type fonts**.
> Click **Next**.
> If you are transferring the presentation to another computer which does not have PowerPoint, activate the **Viewer for Windows 95 or NT** option. If this is not the case, activate **Don't include the viewer**.
> Click **Next**.
>
> *The wizard summarises the actions it is going to carry out.*
>
> Click **Finish**.
>
> *The wizard starts working and displays different messages.*
>
> Click **OK**.
>
> *A message appears on the screen telling you that the presentation has been packed.*
>
> Click **OK** to confirm this message.

Packing a presentation

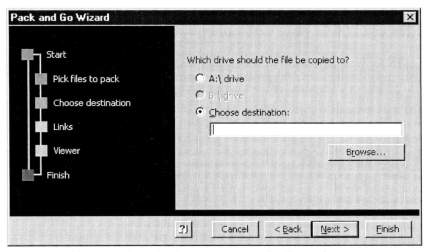

You can select the destination using the **Browse** button.

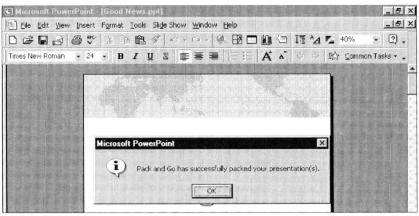

This message tells you that the presentation has been compressed without any problems.

Creating and using slide shows

Unpacking a presentation

Open the Windows Explorer on the computer on which you want to unpack the presentation.

If necessary, create a destination folder for the compressed viewer files.

Be careful, the name of this folder should respect MS-DOS naming rules, meaning it should not exceed 8 characters, and should not contain spaces or punctuation.

Display the contents of the floppy disk.

Double-click the **pngsetup.exe** file.

> In the **Destination Folder** text box, type the name of the folder where the unpacked files are to be placed.
>
> Confirm this choice by clicking **OK**.
>
> *The extraction of the files might take a moment.*
>
> After a brief wait, you are reminded that the viewer does not work under Windows 3.1. Click **OK**.
>
> Once the files have been unpacked, you can choose whether or not to view the presentation straight away by clicking **Yes** or **No**.

Viewing a presentation with the Viewer

In the Windows Explorer, go to the folder that contains the unpacked presentation files.

Double-click the **Ppview32.exe** file to start the viewer.

> Double-click the name of the presentation you want to see.
>
> *The slide show starts almost instantly.*
>
> Let the slide show run.
>
> *At the end of the show, the viewer returns to the screen.*
>
> When you have finished using the viewer, click **Exit**.

Unpacking a presentation

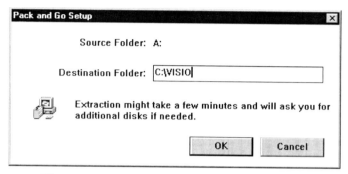

The presentation is going to be unpacked and stored
in the **VISIO** folder.

Viewing a presentation with the Viewer

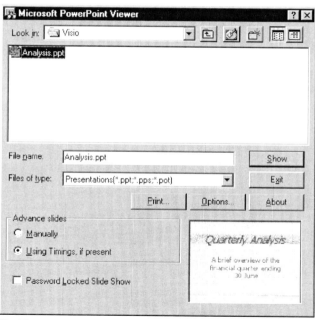

The Viewer lists all the unpacked files it has found and offers
some options concerning the slide show.

Sending a presentation as an attachment

Sending a presentation in this way requires the PowerPoint application to be installed on the recipient's computer. The presentation can be edited and possibly returned and/or kept by the recipient.

Open or create the presentation you want to send.

File - Send To - Mail Recipient (as Attachment)

In the **To** box, type the address(es) of the recipient(s), separating them with a semi-colon, or you can click the **To** button to choose addresses from an address book.

In the **Cc** box, indicate the address of anyone who is to receive a carbon copy of the message.

Type or change the subject of the message in the **Subject** box.

If you want to add a comment, click in the message body area (lower part of the window) so that the insertion point appears, and type your message.

Click **Send**.

To open and edit the attachment, the recipient must first open the message then double-click the corresponding icon. PowerPoint opens and displays the document.

Sending a presentation as an attachment

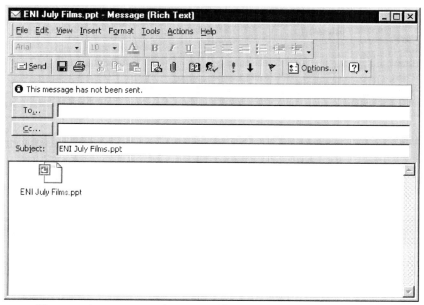

The e-mail message window opens (Outlook in this example). An icon in the lower part of the window represents the document.

Applying a design template

A design template contains formatting elements.

Format - Apply Design Template or

In the **Look in** *list, the* **Presentation Designs** *folder is selected by default.*

 Select the template you want to use.

Click **Apply** or double-click the name of the template.

A design template contains a stylised colour scheme and formatting which replaces those in all the slides in the active presentation.

 Double-clicking the name of the template on the status bar also opens the template list.

Creating a design template

Create a new presentation, or open an existing one.

Insert all the items that are to be included in the template by using the different masters (see chapter 4 - Customising slides using the masters).

File - Save As

If you need to, type the template's name in the **File name** box.
Open the **Save as type** list and choose **Design Template (*.pot)**.

This option opens the **Templates** *folder in the* **Microsoft** *folder.*

 If need be, select a sub-folder in the **Templates** folder.
Click **Save**.

Template files carry the extension .pot.

Applying a design template

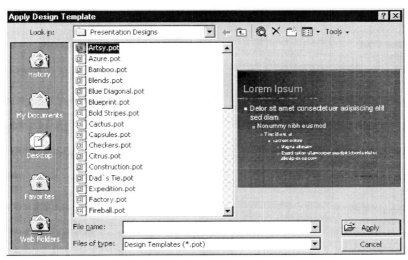

A preview illustrates each template.

Creating a design template

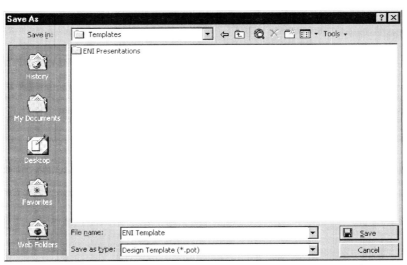

*The design templates saved in this **Templates** folder appear under the **General** tab of the **File - New** dialog box.*

Creating and using slide shows

PERSONAL NOTES

_____

_____

_____

_____

_____

_____

_____

_____

_____

_____

_____

_____

_____

_____

_____

_____

_____

_____

_____

_____

_____

_____

_____

_____

_____

_____

_____

Chapter 3

SLIDE SHOWS

Viewing a slide show

If the slide show has not been timed, you will have to scroll the slides manually.

View - Slide Show or **Slide Show - View Show** or F5

> ✍ If the slides do not scroll automatically: **to see the next slide**, click the slide, type **N** or press Pg Dn , → , ↓ , Enter or space . If the slide contains animations that do not run automatically, these keys will run the animations before they display the next slide.
>
> To go the previous slide, press **P** or Pg Up , ← or ↑ .
>
> *By default, the last slide is a black slide.*
>
> End the slide show by pressing Esc .

 The 🖥 tool starts the slide show from the selected slide.

Viewing a slide show continuously

You will only be able to stop the slide show by pressing Esc .

Slide Show - Set Up Show

> ✍ To run the show continuously without having to restart it, activate the **Loop continuously until 'Esc'** option.
>
> To run the show and have it restart automatically after 5 minutes of inactivity, activate the **Browsed at a kiosk (full screen)** option. This option automatically activates **Loop continuously until 'Esc'**.
>
> Click **OK**.
>
> *Once the slide show finishes, remember to deactivate the selected option in order to return to a standard slide show.*

Viewing a slide show

The buttons at the bottom left of the screen allow you to open the slide show's menu.

Viewing a slide show continuously

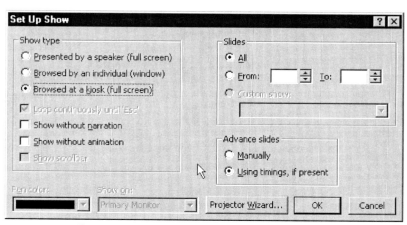

*The **Browsed at a kiosk** option activates and locks the **Loop continuously until 'Esc'** option.*

Automating a slide show

To define the display time for each slide, go to Slide Sorter view and select the slides that are to have the same display time.

Slide Show - Slide Transition or on the **Slide Sorter** toolbar

> Activate the **Automatically after** option and type the selection's display time in the text box underneath this option.
> If you want to keep the option of scrolling the slides manually, activate the **On mouse click** option.
> If all the slides are to have these settings, click **Apply to All**, but of only the current selection is concerned, click **Apply**.
> *The display time of the slides is shown under each miniature.*
> To check the automated scrolling of the slides, use **Slide Show - Set Up Show**, activate the **Use timings, if present** option then click **OK**.

Showing only certain slides

Slide Show - Set Up Show, or hold the ⇧Shift key down and click the button in the bottom left corner of the presentation window.

> In the **Slides** frame, activate the **From** box and type the number of the first slide you want to show.
> Go to the **To** box and type the number of the last slide you want to show.
> Click **OK**.
> Run the slide show with **View - Slide Show**.
> *Be careful, PowerPoint remembers these settings, so think to reselect **All** the slides, if need be.*

When you enter a number in the **From** box, the total number of slides in the presentation automatically appears in the **To** box.

Automating a slide show

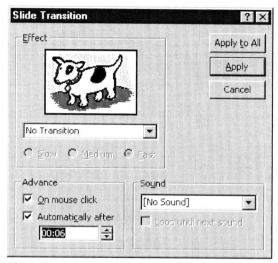

The selected slides will be displayed for 6 seconds.

Showing only certain slides

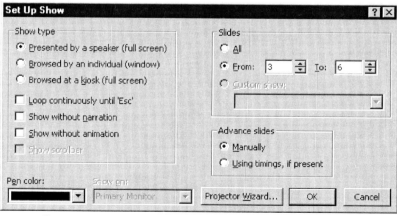

Only slides 3, 4, 5 and 6 from this presentation will be shown.

Going to a particular slide during a show

Start the slide show using **View - Slide Show**.

To go to slide 1 press `Home`.

Press `End` to go to the last slide.

To go to a slide when you know its number, enter its number and confirm with `Enter`.
If you enter a number that does not exist, the last slide is shown systematically.

To go to a slide whose title or number you do not know, move the mouse to make the pointer and the two buttons appear then click one of these buttons to open the Slide Show menu.

Drag the mouse to the **Go** option then the **By Title** option.

Click the title of the slide you want to see.

Showing/hiding a slide during a slide show

Start the slide show using **View - Slide Show**.
Go to the slide you want to hide.

To make the screen white, type **W** or a comma. You can display the slide again with the same keys.

To make the screen black, type **B** or a full-stop. You can display the slide again with the same keys.

Microsoft PowerPoint 2000

Going to a particular slide during a show

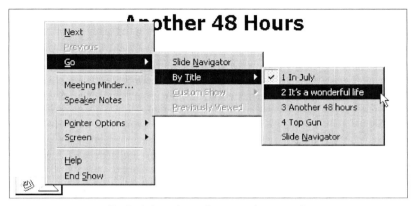

Each slide title is shown with its number.

Showing/hiding a slide during a slide show

The slide is hidden (white screen) and the buttons appear in the bottom left of the screen if you move the mouse.

Making transitions

A transition is the way in which a slide appears on screen during a slide show.

View - Slide Sorter or ▦

Select the slide(s) that will have the same transition.

Slide Show - Slide Transition or ⬜ on the **Slide Sorter** toolbar

    ↳ Click the transition you want in the **Effect** frame.

    Look at the example that PowerPoint shows you.

    If necessary, change the speed of the transition using the **Slow**, **Medium** and **Fast** options.

    To associate a sound with a transition, open the **Sound** drop-down list. If the sound you want is in the list, click it. If not, click the **Other Sound** option and select the sound you want to use.

    Use the **No Sound** option when you want to remove any sound from the transition. If the sound should only play once, leave the **Loop until next sound** option inactive. Activate this option to play the sound continuously until the next sound.

    If only the current selection is concerned by these settings, click **Apply**. If, however, all the slides are concerned, click **Apply to All**.

    The Slide Transition Effects list on the Slide Sorter toolbar allows you to choose an effect, but you cannot change the speed of the effect.

    ↳ To test an effect, go to **Slide Sorter** view then click the ⬜ icon underneath the slide miniature, or click the ▦ tool button.

 You can also apply transitions via the **Slide Show - Slide Transition** menu in the other three views.

Making transitions

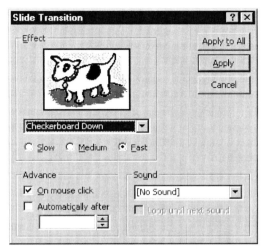

*A preview in the top left of the dialog box
illustrates the selected effect.*

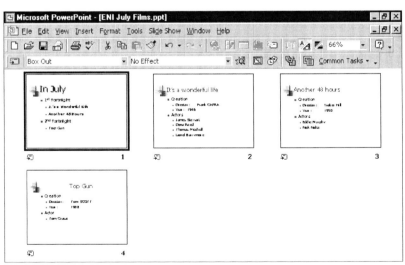

A transition effect has been applied to all the slides in this presentation.

Preventing a sound/video from interrupting a slide show

The following actions apply to sounds or videos inserted into a slide as objects (see chapter 6 - Sounds/Videos). Do you want to stop the slide show while the sound or video is playing?

Activate Normal or Slide view.

Activate the slide concerned then select the video or sound (loudspeaker icon) concerned.

Slide Show - Custom Animation or 📷 on the **Animation Effects** toolbar.

Activate the **Multimedia Settings** tab, if need be, and activate the **Play using animation order** option.

> 🐁 In the **While playing** options, choose whether to **Pause slide show** or **Continue slide show**.
> If you have chosen to **Continue slide show**, indicate whether the sound or video should stop **After current slide** or **After X slides**.
> Activate the **Hide while not playing** check box if you want to hide the loudspeaker (or the video) during the slide show.
> Confirm your choices by clicking **OK**.

Repeating a video/sound

Go to Normal or Slide view.

Activate the slide concerned then select the video or sound object concerned.

If the object is a video, use **Edit - Movie Object**. For a sound, use **Edit - Sound Object**.

> 🐁 Activate the **Loop until stopped** option.
> Click **OK** to confirm.

 Clicking the **More Options** button in the **Multimedia Settings** tab of the **Custom Animation** dialog box can also open the **Options** dialog box.

Microsoft PowerPoint 2000

Preventing a sound/video from interrupting a slide show

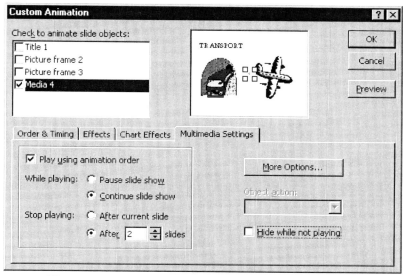

The options in the **Multimedia Settings** tab are only available
if the **Play using animation order** option is active.

Repeating a video/sound

Activate this option to play the movie
or sound continuously until you stop it.

Applying a preset effect

This feature means you can apply preset audio and/or visual effects to the objects in a slide.

In Normal or Slide view, show the **Animation Effects** toolbar by clicking the tool button on the **Formatting** toolbar.

To apply a preset animation effect to titles and body text, activate the slide concerned, and, without selecting anything, click:

 The title appears to fall in from above the slide.

 The body text appears in stages.

To apply a preset animation effect to any object, select the object you want to animate (which can be a title or body text or any other type of object) and, depending on the animation you want, click:

 The object "drives" in from the right accompanied by the noise of a car.

 The object flies in from the left with a whooshing sound.

 The object appears as though seen through a camera shutter accompanied by the sound of a photograph being taken.

 for the object to flash on screen then disappear.

If you are animating text, you might prefer these effects:

 The text flies in letter by letter from the top right of the window.

 The text appears letter by letter accompanied by the noise of a typewriter.

 The text appears from the bottom up. This option is not available for titles.

 The text appears to drop in, word by word, from above the screen.

As soon as an animation effect has been applied to an object, its number is shown in the **Animation Order** *list on the* **Animation Effects** *toolbar.*

 To see a preview of the effect without starting the slide show, click the in Slide Sorter view.

Applying a preset effect

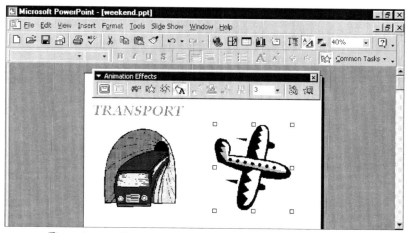

The selected object is the third animated object in this slide.

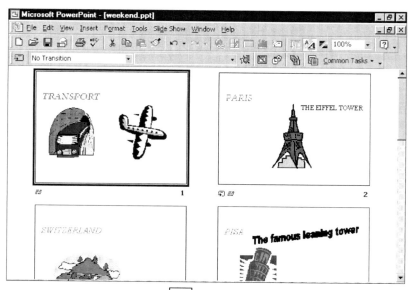

In Slide Sorter view, the ⊞ icon appears under the miniatures
of slides that contain animated objects.

Applying a custom animation effect

Go to Normal or Slide view.

Activate the slide that contains the objects you want to animate.

Slide Show - Custom Animation or click the ▨ tool button on the **Animation Effects** toolbar.

Click the **Effects** tab.

> ☞ For each object in the current slide that you want to animate, proceed as follows:
>
> – Select the object you want to animate in the **Check to animate slide objects** list.
> – In the **Entry animation and sound** frame, select the effect you want in the first list, and the direction in the second.
> – If you want an accompanying sound, select it from the third list in the **Entry animation and sound** frame. You can remove an animation sound by choosing **No Sound**.
> – Click the **Preview** button to see and hear the result.
>
> Click **OK** to confirm these animation settings.

Removing an animation effect

Be in Normal or Slide view.

Activate the slide that contains the object whose animation you want to remove.

Select the object in question.

Slide Show - Preset Animation

> ☞ Click the **Off** option.

Applying a custom animation effect

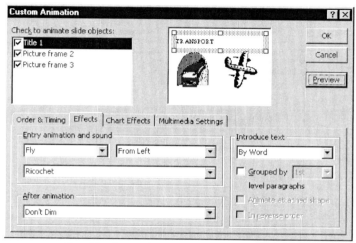

The ***Check to animate slide objects*** *list shows the animated objects in the slide.*

Removing an animation effect

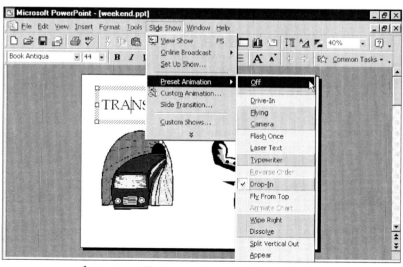

Animation effects are also available in this list.

Creating and using slide shows

Automating an animation

If you automate your animations they will run automatically during a slide show. If you do not, you will have to press the space *bar* Enter *,* → *,* ↓ *,* Pg Dn *or N to run them.*

In Normal or Slide view, activate the slide that contains the objects whose animation you want to automate.

Slide Show - Custom Animation or click the 🖼 tool button on the **Animation Effects** toolbar. Click the **Order & Timing** tab.

> ↳ Select the object concerned in the **Animation order** frame.
>
> In the **Start animation** frame, click the **Automatically** option.
>
> Indicate the number of seconds that will separate this animation from the next in the text box underneath the **Automatically** option.
>
> Confirm by clicking **OK**.
>
> *If the animation is a sound or movie, it must finish playing before the slide show will continue.*

Changing the animation order

In Normal or Slide view, activate the slide that contains the animated objects.

To change the animation order of several objects, use **Slide Show - Custom Animation** or click the 🖼 tool button on the **Animation Effects** toolbar.

> ↳ In the **Animation order** list, select the object you want to move.
>
> Click the ⬆ or ⬇ tool button. Do this for every object you want to move in the animation order.
>
> Click **OK** to confirm.

 To change the animation order object by object, select the object in question, open the **Animation Order** list on the **Animation Effects** toolbar, and click the appropriate number in the order.

Microsoft PowerPoint 2000

Automating an animation

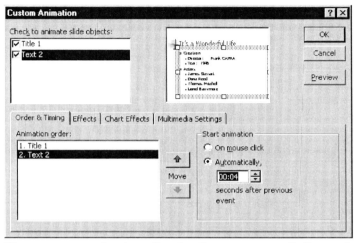

*The animation on the object **Text 2** will run automatically 4 seconds after the animation of **Title 1**.*

Changing the animation order

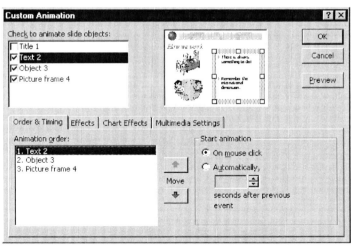

*The **Text 2** object is going to moved in the animation order. You can see the selected object in the preview box.*

Managing the order in which text appears

You can manage the way in which text appears. It can appear paragraph by paragraph, word by word, or in reverse order, for example.

Go to Normal or Slide view.

Activate the slide that contains the text in question.

Slide Show - Custom Show or click the ⬚ tool button on the **Animation Effects** toolbar.

Select the text object in question in the **Check to animate slide objects** list and click the **Effects** tab.

> Open the first list in the **Introduce text** frame and choose how you want to introduce the text: **All at once**, **By Word** and **By Letter**.
>
> Depending on what you want to do, activate or deactivate the following options:

Grouped by X level paragraphs	to introduce the text one group of paragraphs at a time (how the paragraphs are grouped depends on the level selected in the list box).
In reverse order	to have the last line(s) of the text in the selected level appear first.
Animate attached shape	when an AutoShape contains text, activating this option will animate the text and the shape as a single object.

If necessary, click the **Preview** button to see the result.

Click **OK** to confirm.

Managing the order in which text appears

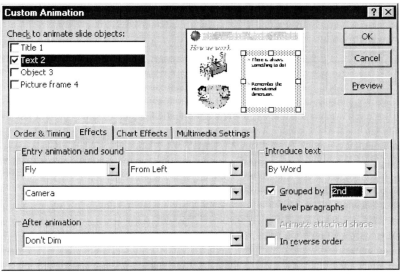

The *In reverse order* option is only available if the *Grouped by X level paragraph* option is active.

PERSONAL NOTES

Chapter 4

SLIDES

■ **MANAGING SLIDES** p.78

Creating a new slide

Activate the slide that will precede the new slide.

Insert - New Slide or 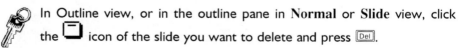 or Ctrl **M**

This command can be used whichever view you are in.

> Choose the layout you want.
>
> Click **OK**.
>
> *A blank slide appears instantly. Its number is shown on the left of the status bar.*
>
> When the insertion point is in the body text, you can create a new slide by pressing Ctrl Enter. PowerPoint creates a new slide with the same layout as the slide you are in, except if this is a **Title Slide**.
>
> **To create a slide at the beginning of a presentation**, go to **Normal** view ( ) then click in the Outline pane before slide number 1 (a vertical line indicates the insertion point to the left of the slide). Use **Insert - New Slide** (or Ctrl **M**) then choose and confirm the slide layout.

Deleting slides

In Normal or Slide view, activate the slide you want to delete and use **Edit - Delete Slide**.

> **In Slide Sorter view** (**View - Slide Sorter**), select the slides you want to delete then use **Edit - Clear** or press Del on the keyboard.

In Outline view, or in the outline pane in **Normal** or **Slide** view, click the icon of the slide you want to delete and press Del.

Creating a new slide

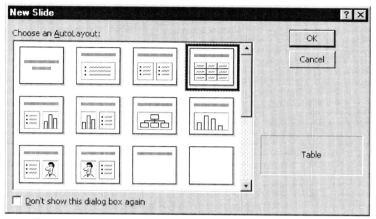

The name of the selected slide layout is shown in the lower
right part of the window.

Deleting slides

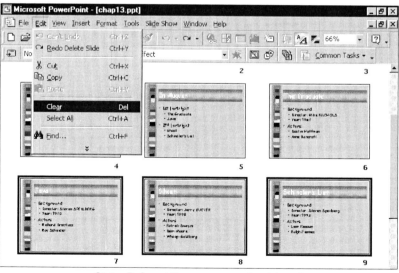

Slides 7, 8 and 9 are going to be deleted.

Changing the layout applied to a slide

Activate the slide concerned.

Format - Slide Layout or ▣

> ✍ You can also click the **Slide Layout** option from the list on the **Common Tasks** button. Double-click the layout you want, or select it and click **Apply**.

Customising slides using the masters

The slide master allows you to change the appearance of all the slides in a presentation. The title master is used to change all the title slides.

View - Master

Click the **Title Master** option if you want to define the appearance of the slides with the **Title Slide** layout, or **Slide Master** to change the presentation of all the other slides.

The status bar reminds you that you are in the Title Master or the Slide Master, and the Master toolbar and a Slide Miniature appear.

> ✍ Make the changes you want. You can add objects, change the fonts, modify the shape of existing items, change the background, and so on. If necessary, open the slide miniature by clicking the ▣ tool button on the **Master** toolbar.
>
> To close the title or slide master, click **Close** on the **Master** toolbar, or activate the view of your choice.

 Hold the [⇧ Shift] key down and click the ▣ button to open the title master (if the current slide has a **Title** layout) or the slide master (when the current slide has another layout).

Changing the layout applied to a slide

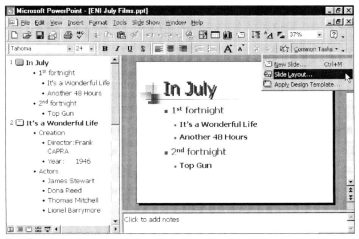

The **Common Tasks** button provides quick access to common features.

Customising slides using the masters

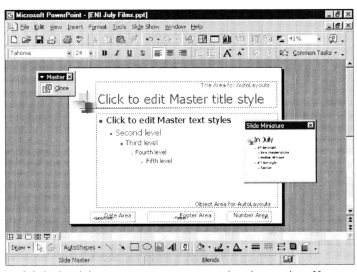

With the slide miniature, you can immediately see the effect
of your changes on the presentation.

Creating and using slide shows

Applying a custom background

If only certain slides are concerned, select them in **Slide Sorter** view. If not, activate any slide.

Format - Background

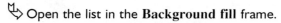 Open the list in the **Background fill** frame.

Click one of the colours offered, or the **More Colors** or **Fill Effects** options to make another choice. If only the selected slide is concerned, click **Apply**. If all the slides in the presentation are concerned, click **Apply to All**.

If you apply a background to all the slides in the presentation, it is also applied to the slide and title masters.

Numbering the slides

If need be, select the slides you want to number in **Slide Sorter** view, or activate any slide.

View - Header and Footer

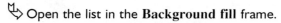 In the **Slide** tab, activate the **Slide number** option.

Activate the **Don't show on title slide** option if you do not want any slide with a Title Slide layout to be numbered.

If only the current selection is concerned, click **Apply**. If all the slides are to be numbered, click **Apply to All**.

The slide numbers are shown in the bottom right of the slides.

Applying a custom background

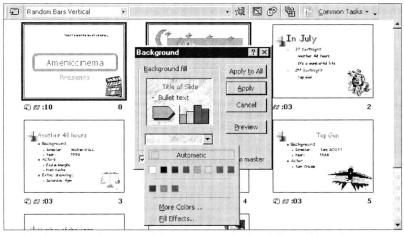

The Automatic button enables you to apply the slide and/or title master
background, so long as a custom background has not been applied
to the slides in the presentation.

Numbering the slides

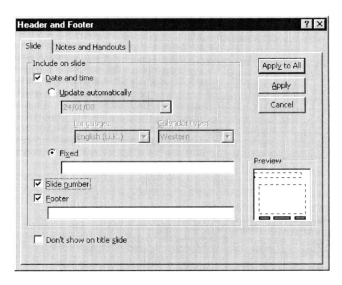

Applying a colour scheme

If you only want to apply a colour scheme to certain slides, activate **Slide Sorter** view and select them. If not, activate any slide.

Format - Slide Color Scheme

If need be, click the **Standard** tab.

> ↳ Select the colour scheme you want to use.
>
> *The colour schemes in the* **Color schemes** *frame are linked to the current template.*
>
> Click **Apply** to apply the colours to the current selection, or **Apply to All** if the change is destined for all the slides and the corresponding master.

Sending a slide as the body of a message

This feature means that the recipient can see the contents of a slide even if they do not have PowerPoint installed on their computer.

Open or create the presentation then go to the slide you want to send.

File - Send To - Mail Recipient or 🖃

Click **Send the current slide as the message body** and confirm.

A new toolbar appears, followed by three text boxes.

> ↳ In the **To** box, type the address(es) of the recipient(s), separating their names with semi-colons or click the 📖 To... button to select addresses from an address book.
>
> In the **Cc** box, enter the address(es) of anyone to whom you want to send a carbon copy of the message.
>
> In the **Subject** box, type your message's subject. The name of the document appears here by default.
>
> Click the **Send this Slide** button.
>
> *A copy is sent to the recipient(s). The slide is the message body.*

Applying a colour scheme

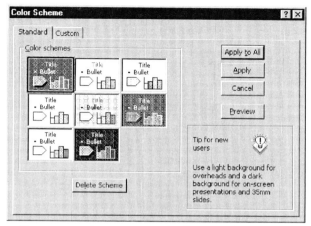

You can use the options on the **Custom** tab to create
your own colour scheme.

Sending a slide as the body of a message

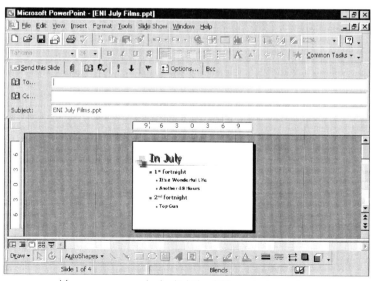

You screen may look slightly different, depending
on your e-mail application (Microsoft Outlook here).

PERSONAL NOTES

Chapter 5

TEXT

Entering a slide title

Go to Normal or Slide view.

Activate the slide whose title you want to enter.
Click in the title placeholder, where the text **Click to add title** appears.
A frame with a hatched border replaces the message.

> Type the title, using Enter to insert line breaks, if you need to.
> Confirm the text by pressing Esc, or click outside of the title placeholder.

Entering slide body text

Go to Normal or Slide view.

Activate the slide in question.
Click in the body text placeholder where the text **Click to add text** appears. If the insertion point is in the title, press Ctrl Enter to go to the text placeholder.

The body of the slide becomes a frame with a hatched border in which the insertion point appears.

Enter the text, keeping these points in mind:

− Enter text without worrying about the ends of lines, only press Enter to go to the next point.
− To insert tab stops at the beginning of a line, press Ctrl Alt ⇄.
− Press ⇧ Shift Enter to create empty lines.

> You can define the hierarchy of your lists by placing the insertion point at the beginning of the line and pressing ⇄ or ➡ to go to the level below, or ⇧ Shift ⇄ or ⬅ to step one level above.
>
> If necessary, finish entering the text by pressing Esc or click outside the text placeholder.
>
> *All the text entered in the title and text placeholders appears in the presentation's outline. PowerPoint has six outline levels: the title and five levels in the body text.*

Entering a slide title

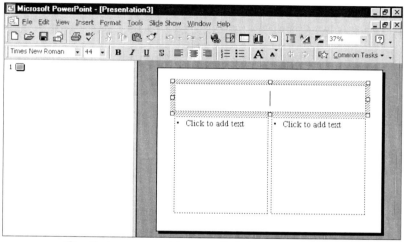

The flashing vertical line is called the insertion point.

Entering slide body text

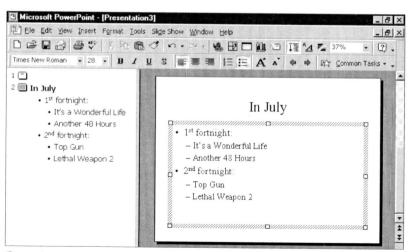

Depending on the level applied to the text, the character size and the symbol at the beginning of the line changes. The different paragraphs are indented in relation to each other.

Entering text in the notes page

View - Notes Page

Activate the slide concerned.

Change the zoom if you need to.

Click in the area called **Click to add notes**.

✎ Type the notes without worrying about the ends of the lines.

 Press ⇄ to insert a tab stop at the beginning of a line.

Modifying text

Click in the text item you want to modify.

To add characters, place the insertion point where they are to appear and type.

To delete a character, press Del if the insertion point is before the character or ← if it is after the character.

To delete a word, press Ctrl Del if the insertion point is before the word and Ctrl ← if it is after.

To delete a group of characters, select them and press Del.

To replace a group of characters, select them and type the new text.

Entering text in the notes page

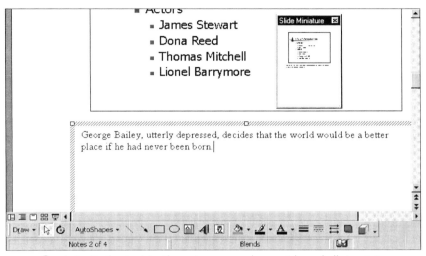

By default, the text in the notes pages does not have bullet points.

Modifying text

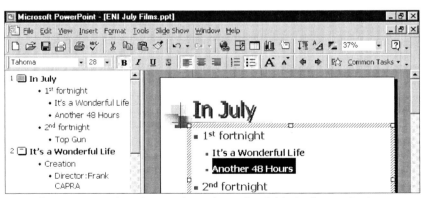

The colour of the selection depends on the slide's background colour.

T E X T

Moving the insertion point in a text object

Click in the text object in question.

Move the insertion point around a text object with the following keys:

→/←	next/previous character.
Ctrl → /Ctrl ←	next/previous word.
Home /End	start/end of the line.
↓/↑	next/previous line.
Ctrl ↓ /Ctrl ↑	start of next/previous paragraph.
Ctrl Home /Ctrl End	start/end of text.

 Apart from the Ctrl ←, Ctrl →, Ctrl ↓ and Ctrl ↑ combinations, use the same keys to move around in the **Outline** pane.

Selecting characters

Click in the text object in question.

To select a word, double-click it.

To select a paragraph, triple-click it.

To select a group of characters, drag the mouse pointer over the characters or click before the first character, point after the last, press ⇧ Shift and click.

All these methods can be used in the Outline pane.

To select the whole text object, use **Edit - Select All** or press Ctrl **A**.

To select all the characters using the keyboard, press the ⇧ Shift key and use the arrow keys.

Moving the insertion point in a text object

The insertion point has been moved to the beginning of the text
with the `Ctrl` `Home` key combination.

Selecting characters

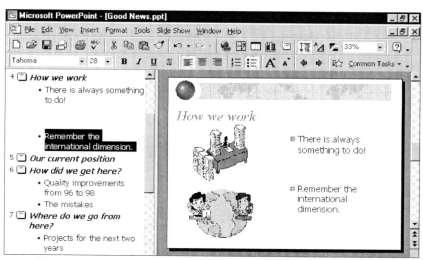

This paragraph was selected in the Outline pane using a triple-click.

TEXT

Checking the spelling in a presentation

Place the insertion point where the spelling check is to start.

Tools - Spelling or or F7

The spelling check starts. PowerPoint reads the words and checks whether they are in its dictionary and a personal dictionary. If the word is unknown to PowerPoint, it appears in the Not in Dictionary box.

☞ **If the word is misspelled**:
- if the correct spelling of the word is in the **Suggestions** list, double-click the work (or click the **Change** button once).
- if you know the correct spelling, type the correct word in the **Change to** box then click **Change**.
- if you want the same mistake to be corrected automatically throughout the document, type the correct word in the **Change to** box then click **Change All**.

If the word is not misspelled:
- click **Ignore** to leave the word unchanged and continue the check.
- click **Ignore All** to skip the word each time it appears during the check.
- click **Add** if you want to add the word to the personal dictionary, whose name is shown in the **Add words to** list.

☞ At the end of the spelling check, a message appears. Click **OK**.

Checking the spelling in a presentation

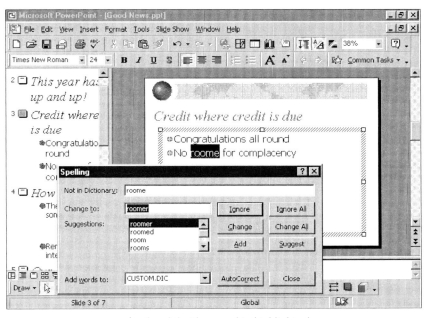

In the slide, the word is highlighted.

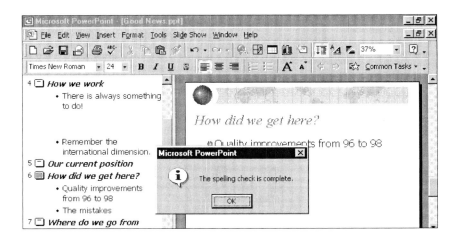

Creating and elaborating slides in Outline view

Click the ▤ button in the bottom left of the presentation window.

For each slide:

- Type the title then go to the contents of the bulleted list by pressing Ctrl Enter , or create a new slide by pressing Enter .
- Type the body text as you would in **Normal** or **Slide** view: press Enter to go to the next line and create a new slide with Ctrl Enter .

[☞] The outline can also be seen in the Outline pane in Normal view.

Changing the display in Outline view

Click the ▤ button at the bottom left of the presentation window.

Activate **View - Toolbars** and select **Outlining** to show the corresponding toolbar.

To show or hide text formatting, activate or deactivate the ▤ tool button on the **Outlining** toolbar.

The different fonts, sizes, formatting and bullets are no longer visible when this tool is deactivated.

[☞] To see all the **text**, or only certain titles, depending on what you want to see, use the following tools:

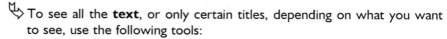

    to see only the titles.

    to see all the titles and text.

You can also use these tools:

    to hide the text linked to the title in which the insertion point is placed.

    to show the text linked to the title in which the insertion point is placed.

Hiding the text so that you can only see the titles can be very useful when you are reorganising your outlines. When you move a title, you are actually moving the slide and all its text.

Creating and elaborating slides in Outline view

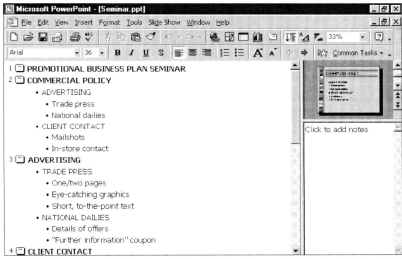

The structure of the presentation appears on the screen, and you can see the slide and notes in the right of the screen.

Changing the display in Outline view

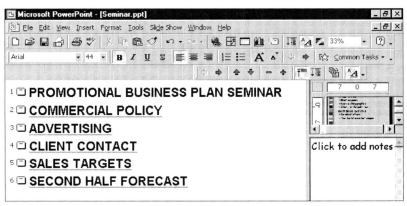

Only the titles can be seen. An underlined title indicates that text, which is currently hidden, is linked to the title.

Creating and using slide shows

Moving paragraphs in Outline view

Click the [≡] button or activate the Outline pane in **Normal** view.

Place the insertion point in the paragraph you want to move. If it is a title with associated text, collapse it by clicking [−].

To move paragraphs using the tools on the Outlining toolbar, use the [⬆] tool button to move the paragraph up or the [⬇] tool button to move the paragraph down.

To move paragraphs by dragging, point to the bullet at the beginning of the line you want to move. When the pointer takes the shape of a four-headed arrow you can drag the paragraph to its new position.

🖑 Release the mouse when you reach the paragraph's new position.

Moving paragraphs in Outline view

The text will be moved to the position of the horizontal line.

Changing the character font

Go to Normal or Slide view.

You can also change the font in Outline view (**).

Select the text item or characters concerned. If the font change concerns all the paragraphs of the same level, go to the slide master and click in the corresponding paragraph.

Open the **Font** drop-down list on the **Formatting** toolbar.

> Click the name of the font you want to use. Try to use fonts preceded by a TT symbol, as these are True Type fonts that are entirely managed by Windows.
>
> *You can also change the font via* ***Format - Font***.

Changing the character size

Go to Normal or Slide view.

Select the text item or characters concerned. If the change in the character size concerns all the paragraphs of the same level, go to the slide master and click the corresponding paragraph.

To increase or decrease the character size, click one of the following buttons:

    to apply the next size up from the one shown in the **Font Size** box.

    to apply the next size down from the one shown in the **Font Size** box.

> If you want to choose an exact size, open the **Font Size** drop-down list on the **Formatting** toolbar.
>
> Click the font size you want, or type a value, remembering to confirm afterwards with Enter .
>
> *The font size can also be changed via* ***Format - Font***.

Changing the character font

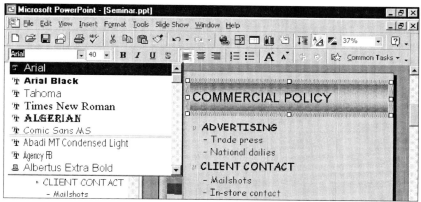

*Fonts are shown in alphabetical order, with the last fonts used
at the top of the list.*

Changing the character size

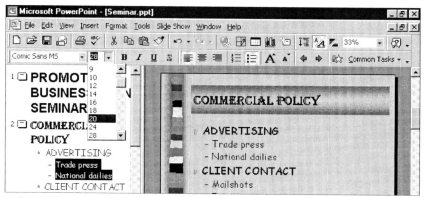

PowerPoint lists the available sizes for the font of the selected characters.

Formatting characters

In Normal, Slide or Outline view, select the text object or characters concerned. If the formatting concerns all the paragraphs of the same level, go to the slide master and click in the corresponding paragraph.

> Click the button(s) on the **Formatting** toolbar that correspond to the formatting you want to apply, or use one of the shortcut key combinations.

B or Ctrl B	**Bold** characters
I or Ctrl I	*Italic* characters
U or Ctrl U	Underlined characters

To remove formatting, click the appropriate tool again.

You can format text as you type it: activate the format, type the text, and then deactivate the format before you continue.

Formatting characters

In Normal, Slide or Outline view, select the text object or characters concerned. If the formatting concerns all the paragraphs of the same level, go to the slide master and click in the corresponding paragraph.

Format - Font

This dialog box contains all the formatting options for characters.

> In the **Font style** list, and the **Effects** frame, activate the formatting you want to apply.

The Offset text box allows you to enter the value by which the text should be slightly above or below the base line. A positive value activates the Superscript option, a negative one the Subscript option.

Confirm your choices by clicking **OK**.

The quickest way to cancel all formatting applied to characters is to use the Ctrl ⇧ Shift **Z** and Ctrl space keyboard shortcuts.

Microsoft PowerPoint 2000

Formatting characters

The selected characters take on the chosen formatting,
and the active tool appears pressed in.

Formatting characters

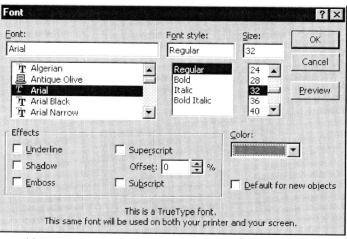

You can use the *Color* drop-down list to choose a colour
for the selected text.

Applying colour to text

In Normal or Slide view, select the text object or characters concerned. If the formatting concerns all the paragraphs of the same level, go to the slide master and click in the corresponding paragraph.

You can also apply colour to text in Outline view.

Open the **Font Color** list ![A] on the **Drawing** toolbar.

⇨ Click one of the colour tabs offered. To select another colour, click the **More Font Colors** option. Activate the **Standard** tab, click the colour you want to use, and then confirm with **OK**.

The chosen colour is added to the list on the ![A] *tool.*

You can also choose text colours via **Format - Font**.

Applying a shadow effect to text

In Normal or Slide view, select the text object or characters concerned. If the formatting concerns all the paragraphs of the same level, go to the slide master and click in the corresponding paragraph.

You can also apply a shadow to text in Outline view.

⇨ Click the ![S] tool button on the **Formatting** toolbar.

If you want to apply a more distinct shading, click the ![button] tool button on the **Drawing** toolbar.

The five options that are not grey are the only ones available for text items. The **No Shadow** *option removes any shading.*

Click the shadow style you want to use.

Click in the slide to deselect the text and see the result.

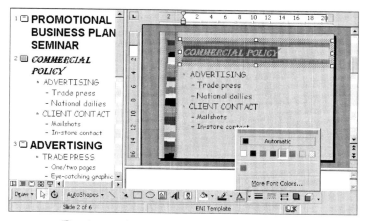

The **Automatic** option restores the default colour.

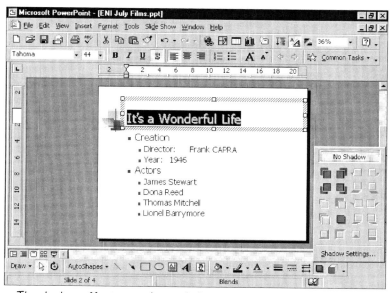

The shadow effect you select only becomes visible when you activate
another object in the slide.

Creating and using slide shows

Changing the bullets

Go to Normal or Slide view.

You can also change the bullets in Outline view.

Select the text concerned. If this change concerns all the paragraphs of the same level, go to the slide master and click in the paragraph concerned.

Format - Bullets and Numbering

If need be, activate the **Bullets** tab.

Select one of the bullet styles on offer. If you want to choose a different bullet, click the **Character** button.

 If necessary, change the bullet font in the **Bullets from** list.

Click the symbol you want to use.

If need be, open the **Color** list and choose a new colour. You can also change the size of the bullet as a percentage of the text size in the **Size as % of text** box.

Confirm by clicking **OK**.

Showing/hiding bullets

Go to Normal or Slide view.

You can also show or hide bullets in Outline view.

Select the text concerned. If this change concerns all the paragraphs of the same level, go to the slide master and click in the paragraph concerned.

Click the tool button.

This tool shows and hides the bullets.

 You can also use **Format - Bullets and Numbering** and activate the **None** option if you want to hide the bullets.

Changing the bullets

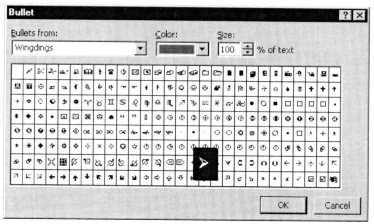

The zoom increases when you click a symbol.

Showing/hiding bullets

The bullet associated with the selected paragraph is hidden.

Changing the text alignment

Go to Normal or Slide view.

You can also change the text alignment when you are in Outline view.

Select all the paragraphs that are to have the same alignment or click in the paragraph you want to align. If this change concerns all the paragraphs of the same level, go to the slide master and click in the paragraph concerned.

↳ On the **Formatting** toolbar, click the tool that corresponds to the alignment you want, or use the keyboard shortcut:

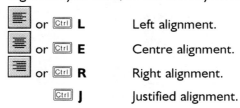

or Ctrl **L**	Left alignment.
or Ctrl **E**	Centre alignment.
or Ctrl **R**	Right alignment.
Ctrl **J**	Justified alignment.

 The **Format - Alignment** command also gives access to the alignments.

Changing the paragraph spacing

Go to Normal or Slide view.

You can also change the paragraph spacing when you are in Outline view.

Select the paragraphs concerned. If this change concerns all the paragraphs of the same level, go to the slide master and click in the appropriate paragraph.
Format - Line Spacing

↳ Choose the unit of measurement you want to use in the **Before paragraph** and **After paragraph** frames.
Enter the value for the spacing before and/or after the paragraph in the corresponding text boxes.
Confirm by clicking **OK**.

 Click the **Preview** button to see the effect of your changes before applying them.

Changing the text alignment

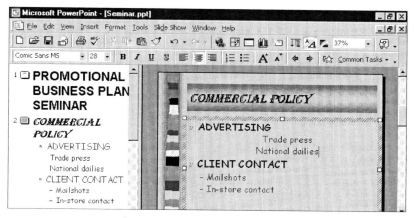

Two paragraphs have been centred.

Changing the paragraph spacing

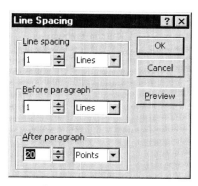

The unit of measurement
can be *Lines* or *Points*.

109

Changing the line spacing

Go to Normal or Slide view.

You can also change the line spacing in Outline view.

Select the paragraphs that are to have the same line spacing. If this change concerns all the paragraphs of the same level, go to the slide master and click in the paragraph concerned.

Format - Line Spacing

> In the **Line spacing** frame, select the unit to use then type the spacing you want in the appropriate text box.
>
> Confirm your choice by clicking **OK**.

Applying paragraph indents

This action will offset text in relation to the left and/or right borders of the text placeholder.

Go to Normal or Slide view.

You can also apply paragraph indents in Outline view.

Display the ruler using **View - Ruler**.

Click in the text object to which you want to apply paragraph indents. If all the paragraphs of the same level are concerned, go to the slide master and click the paragraph concerned.

Place the mouse pointer on the indent marker you want to change.

> Click the indent marker and drag it along the ruler to the required position.

 You can increase the zoom to make this action easier.

Changing the line spacing

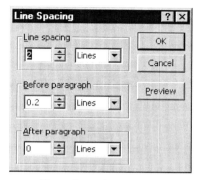

*The selected paragraphs
have a line spacing of 2 Lines.*

Applying paragraph indents

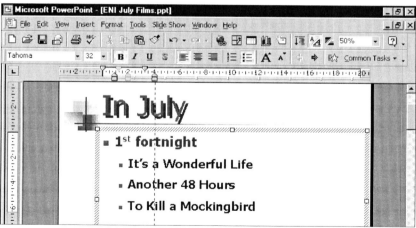

Two indent markers on the ruler manage each outline level.

PERSONAL NOTES

Chapter 6

CREATING OBJECTS

CREATING OBJECTS

Inserting a table

Go to Normal or Slide view.

Place the insertion point where you want to insert the table.

Insert - Table

> Indicate the **Number of columns** and the **Number of rows** in the corresponding text boxes.
> Click **OK**.
>
> *The table appears in the document, at the point where the insertion point is.*

> You can also insert a table by clicking the ⬚ tool button on the **Standard** toolbar, or by double-clicking the placeholder in a slide with a **Table** layout.

Inserting a table

Go to Normal or Slide view.

If necessary, open the **Tables and Borders** toolbar by clicking the ⊞ tool button.

Click the ✎ tool button to activate it.
The mouse pointer becomes a pencil.

Choose the style, weight and colour of the line then drag in the slide to draw the table's external borders.

> If you want to, change the style, weight and colour of the line using the tools on the **Tables and Borders** toolbar, and then draw the internal rows and columns.
>
> Click the ✎ tool button again to deactivate it.

> To move a table, point to one of its edges until the mouse pointer takes this shape: ⊞, and then drag the table to move it.

Inserting a table

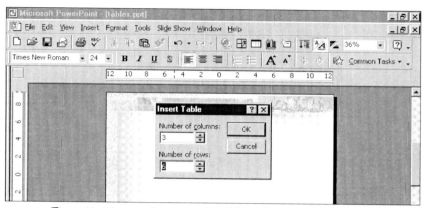

The table about to be inserted will have 3 columns and 6 rows.

Inserting a table

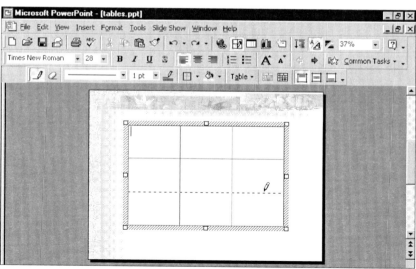

The pointer takes the shape of a pencil, and a dotted line shows
where the line will appear.

Creating and using slide shows

Entering data into a table

Go to Normal or Slide view.

Activate the cell that will contain the data.

Enter the cell's contents as you would type a paragraph.

Go to the next cell and continue.

> You can insert tab stops inside a table by using the ruler, as with a slide. To go to a tab stop, press Ctrl ⇄.

 Format the contents of cells as you would paragraphs.

Moving the insertion point in a table

With the mouse, point to where you want to go and click.

On the keyboard, use the following keys:

| ⇄ or ⇧ Shift ⇄ | Cell to the right or to the left. |
| ↓ or ↑ | Cell above or below. |

Entering data into a table

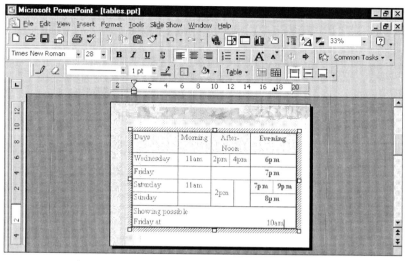

A centred tab stop has been inserted into this table.

Moving the insertion point in a table

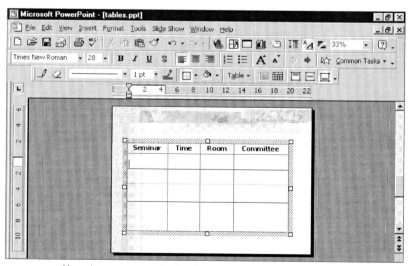

Use the mouse or the keyboard to move around a table.

Creating and using slide shows

Selecting in a table

Go to Normal or Slide view.

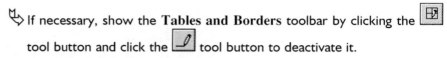

 If necessary, show the **Tables and Borders** toolbar by clicking the tool button and click the tool button to deactivate it.

To select a CELL, click inside the cell (the pointer takes the shape of a vertical line). If you want to select several cells, drag over them.

You can also use ⇄ and ⇧Shift ⇄ on the keyboard.

To select a COLUMN, place the mouse above the column (it takes the shape of a black arrow pointing downwards) and click.

You can also activate a cell in the column, click the Table ▾ button on the Tables and Borders toolbar and choose Select Column.

To select a ROW, activate a cell in the row, click the Table ▾ button on the **Tables and Borders** toolbar and choose **Select Row**.

To select the whole TABLE, select the first cell, hold down the ⇧Shift key, and click in the last cell.

You can also activate a cell in the table, click the Table ▾ button and choose Select Table.

Click in any cell to cancel a selection.

Selecting in a table

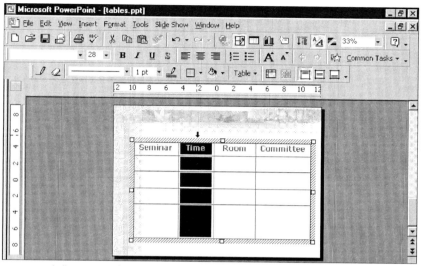

When you select a column, the mouse becomes a black arrow.

Inserting a column

Go to Normal or Slide view.

If you need to, show the **Tables and Borders** toolbar by clicking the ⊞ tool button.

Select a cell in the column after which you want insert a new column.

Click the Table ▾ button on the **Tables and Borders** toolbar and activate the **Insert Columns to the Left** or **Insert Columns to the Right** option.

Inserting a row

Go to Normal or Slide view.

Select a cell in the row after which you want to insert a new row.

Click the Table ▾ button on the **Tables and Borders** toolbar and activate the **Insert Rows Above** or **Insert Rows Below** option.

Inserting a column

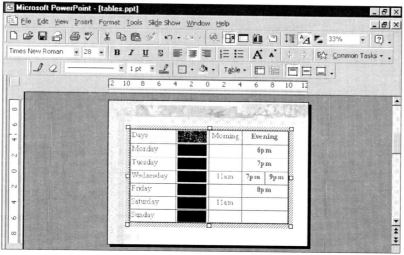

The new column has the same characteristics as the column
you selected initially.

Inserting a row

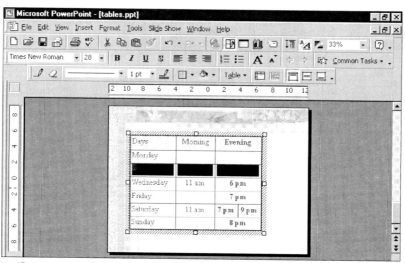

The new row has the same characteristics as the row that was active
at the time of insertion.

Creating and using slide shows

Deleting a row/a column

Go to Normal or Slide view.

If you need to, show the **Tables and Borders** toolbar by clicking the [■] tool button.

Click in a cell in the row or column you want to delete.

🖑 Click the Table ▾ button.

Choose **Delete Rows** or **Delete Columns**.

Changing the width of columns and the height of rows

Go to Normal or Slide view.

Point to the vertical line <u>to the right</u> of the column you want to change, or the horizontal line underneath the row you want to change.

The mouse becomes a double black arrow.

🖑 Drag the mouse to the required width or height.

 You can adjust the width of a column to fit its contents by double-clicking the vertical line to the right of the column.

Tables

Deleting a row/a column

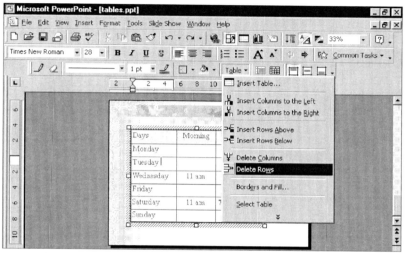

The Tuesday row, where the insertion point is, will be deleted.

Changing the width of columns and the height of rows

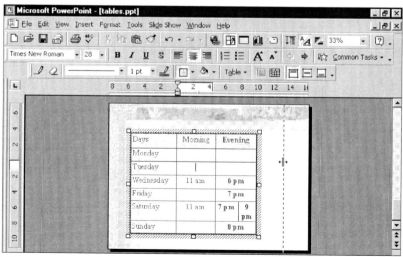

When you change the width of a column, a dotted line indicates its new width.

Creating and using slide shows

Changing a table's borders

Go to Normal or Slide view.

Select the cells concerned, or the whole table.

If necessary, show the **Tables and Borders** toolbar by clicking the ⊞ tool button.

Choose the style [＿＿＿＿＿＿ ▾], weight [½ ▾] and colour [✎] of the line.

⇩ Open the [▢ ▾] list and choose the borders you want to apply:

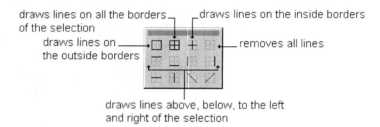

draws lines on all the borders of the selection   draws lines on the inside borders

draws lines on the outside borders   removes all lines

draws lines above, below, to the left and right of the selection

Merging cells

This action allows you to transform several cells into one.

Go to Normal or Slide view.

If you need to, show the **Tables and Borders** toolbar by clicking ⊞.

Select the cells you want to merge.

⇩ Click the ⊞ button on the **Tables and Borders** toolbar.

🔑 You can also click the ✐ button on the **Tables and Borders** toolbar to erase the line that separates the cells you want to merge by dragging the pointer along the line in question.

Changing a table's borders

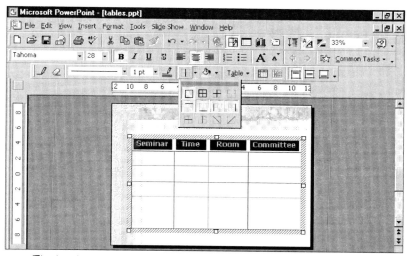

The borders you have chosen are applied only to the selected cells.

Merging cells

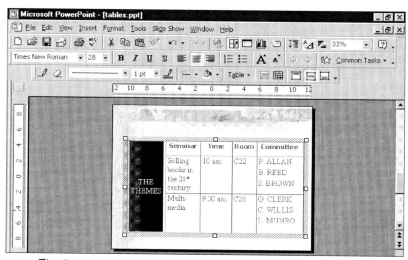

The first cells of the three rows in this table have been merged.

Creating and using slide shows

Splitting cells

This technique means you can split one cell into several.

Go to Normal or Slide view.

Show the **Tables and Borders** toolbar if you need to by clicking the ⊞ tool button.

Select the cell(s) you want to split.

↳ Click the ⊞ tool button on the **Tables and Borders** toolbar.

Changing the vertical alignment of a cell

Go to Normal or Slide view.

If you need to, show the **Tables and Borders** toolbar by clicking the ⊞ tool button.

Select the cell(s) whose alignment you want to change.

↳ Click the tool on the bar which corresponds to what you want to do:

⊟ to align the text at the top of the cell,

⊟ to align the text in the middle of the cell,

⊟ to align the text at the bottom of the cell.

Splitting cells

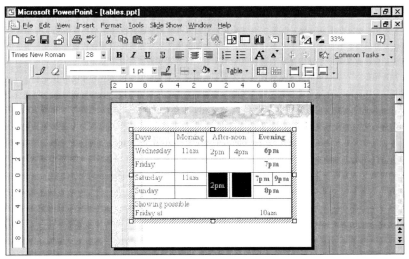

The selected cell has been split in two.

Changing the vertical alignment of a cell

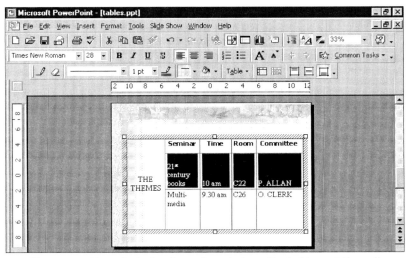

The text in the selected cells is aligned along the bottom of the cell.

Inserting a picture from the Clip Gallery

Go to Normal or Slide view.

Activate the slide concerned.

In slides with a **Text & Clip Art** or **Clip Art & Text** layout, double-click the place-holder called **Double click to add clip art**.

For slides with any other layout, or if you want to add a picture to a slide that already contains one, use **Insert - Picture - Clip Art** or click this tool button: ▨.

Depending on how PowerPoint has been installed, you might be asked to insert the Office 2000 CD-ROM into the drive. If the CD-ROM is in the drive, more clips are available.

    Activate the **Pictures** or **Motion Clips** tab, depending on what you want to insert.

    Different categories appear on the screen.

    Click the category that corresponds to what you want, or search for a picture by typing keywords in the **Search for clips** text box and confirm with Enter .

    To see the previous group of clips, click ⬅, and to see the next group, click ➡.

    Click ▦ to see all the categories.

    You can increase or decrease the size of the window by clicking the ⬛ or ⬛ buttons.

    To insert a picture, click the one you want then click the ⬛ button on the toolbar that appears.

    Click the ☒ button to close the **Insert ClipArt** window.

    You can also click the ⬛ button to reduce the window, and then drag the picture to the desired place in the slide.

Inserting a picture from the Clip Gallery

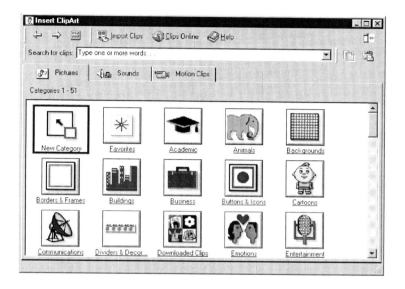

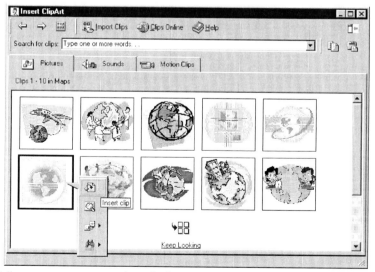

When you point to a tool on the bar, its function appears in a ScreenTip.

Importing a picture from a file

In Normal or Slide view, activate the slide in which you want to insert a picture.

Insert - Picture - From File

Go to the drive that contains the picture you want to import by clicking the black triangle at the right of the **Look in** drop-down list.

This list contains all of the drives you can access from your computer (the disk drive (A:), the hard disk (C:), maybe a CD-ROM and drives on a network (Network Neighborhood)).

⇘ Open the folder that contains the picture you want to import by double-clicking its icon (yellow folder).

The name of the folder is now visible in the Look in box.

To go to the parent folder, click the 🔼 button.

To see a detailed list, open the ▦▾ list and click the **Details** option.

To see the properties of a picture, open the ▦▾ list and click the **Properties** option.

Return to the standard list by choosing List from the ▦▾ menu.

Select the picture you want to import and click **Insert**, or double-click the picture.

 You can also use the 🖼 button on the **Picture** toolbar.

Importing a picture from a file

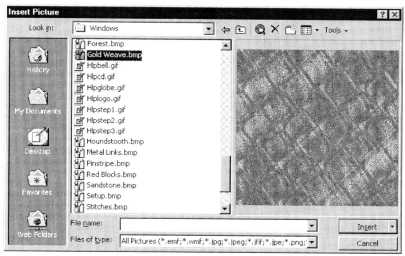

A preview of the picture is shown in the right of the dialog box.

Creating and using slide shows

Inserting a movie clip or sound from the Clip Gallery

Go to Normal or Slide view.

Insert the Microsoft Office 2000 CD-ROM in the drive.

Insert - Picture - Clip Art or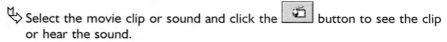
Click the **Motion Clips** or **Sounds** tab.

Select the category that corresponds to the clip you want, or search for a clip by typing keywords in the **Search for clips** box.

> Select the movie clip or sound and click the button to see the clip or hear the sound.
>
> Click the [button] button to insert it into the slide.
>
> Click **Yes** if you want the sound or movie to be played automatically during a slide show.
>
> *Click the* ☒ *button to close the* ***Insert Clip Art*** *window.*

Movies and sounds can also be inserted using **Insert - Movies and Sounds - Movie from Gallery** or **Sound from Gallery**.

Inserting a movie clip or sound from the Clip Gallery

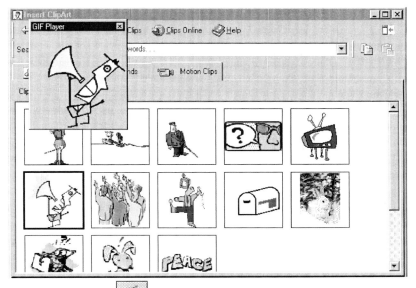

When you click [ ] a GIF Player window opens so that you can see the selected movie clip.

Inserting a movie or sound from a file

In Normal or Slide view, go to the slide concerned.

Insert - Movies and Sounds - Movie from File or Sound from File

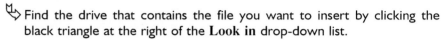 Find the drive that contains the file you want to insert by clicking the black triangle at the right of the **Look in** drop-down list.

Open the folder that contains the movie or sound file you want to insert by double-clicking its icon (yellow folder).

Double-click the file you want to insert, or select it and click **OK**.

Sound objects are represented by a loudspeaker icon.

Managing sound objects

In Normal or Slide view, go to the slide concerned.

To listen to an inserted sound, double-click the loudspeaker that represents it.

If the sound plays for too long, press Esc *to stop it.*

 To hide the loudspeaker, place it behind an object with a fill. If you do not have any objects in your slide, you can create an object with a fill that is the same as the slide's background, and place the loudspeaker behind it.

Inserting a movie or sound from a file

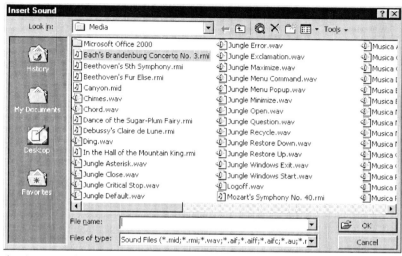

*In this example, you can see the files contained in the **Windows Media** folder.*

Managing sound objects

The loudspeaker is going to be placed behind the object on which it is positioned.

Creating and using slide shows

Drawing an oval/rectangle/straight line/arrow

In Normal or Slide view, activate the slide concerned.

    On the **Drawing** toolbar, click the button that corresponds to what you want to draw:

    to draw a **Line**.

    to draw an **Arrow**.

    to draw a **Rectangle**.

    to draw an **Oval**.

*The **Drawing** toolbar can be shown using* **View - Toolbars - Drawing**.

When you place the mouse pointer in the slide it becomes a black cross. Place this cross where you want to start (or finish) the drawing.

Draw the shape by dragging.

After you have drawn the shape, the object is selected automatically. If you have to draw the same shape several times, double-click the shape tool you want to use, and then draw all the shapes you want before pressing Esc

If you want to draw a square or a circle, use the   and   tools and hold the ⇧ key down as you drag. To draw a rectangle/square or an oval/circle from the centre and not from one corner, hold the Ctrl key down as you drag.

Drawing an oval/rectangle/straight line/arrow

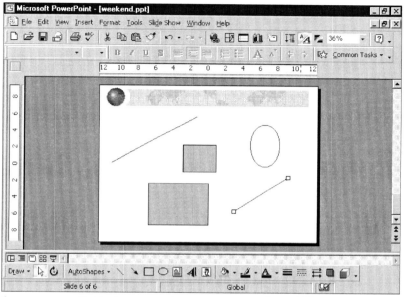

As soon as you finish drawing a shape it appears selected. The colours applied to shapes depend on the colour scheme you are using, which is very often linked to the template.

Drawing an AutoShape

AutoShapes are predefined shapes offered by PowerPoint (stars, bubbles, arrows, cylinders and so on).

In Normal or Slide view, activate the slide concerned.
Open the **AutoShapes** list on the **Drawing** toolbar.

⇲ Point to the category that contains the shape you want.

AutoShapes are stored in eight different categories. Each category has a different number of shapes.

Point to the shape you want to draw and click it to select it.

Draw the shape either by dragging or by clicking to draw a preset shape.

Creating a text box

A text box allows you to place text where you want in a slide.

In Normal or Slide view, go to the slide concerned.

Insert - Text Box or ▦ on the **Drawing** toolbar
The mouse pointer becomes a fine arrow pointing downwards.

If you know how wide you want to the box to be, draw the frame by dragging. If you do not, click in the slide where you want to start the text.

⇲ Type the text in the same way as ordinary paragraphs.
Click outside the text box or press Esc when you have finished.
If the text box does not have the right dimensions, you can resize it by dragging or by changing the information in the **Size** tab after using **Format - Text Box**.

Drawing an AutoShape

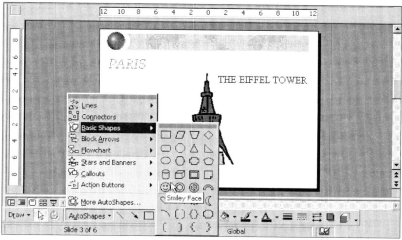

When you point to a shape, its name appears in a ScreenTip.

Creating a text box

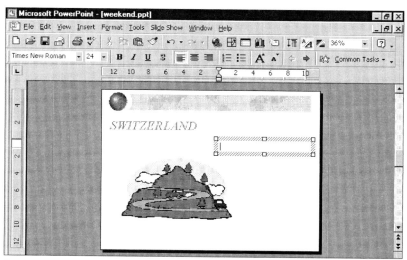

An insertion point appears in the text box, which is shown by a hatched frame.

Creating and using slide shows

Inserting a WordArt object

A WordArt object allows you to present text with different typographical effects.

In Normal or Slide view, activate the slide concerned.

Insert - Picture - WordArt or ▣ (**Drawing** toolbar).
Double-click the effect you want to use, or click it then click **OK**.

ᗏ Type your text, using ⌷Enter⌷insert line breaks.

Use the **Font** and **Size** lists, and the ▣ G ▣ and ▣ I ▣ tool buttons, to format the text.

Click **OK** to confirm.

The text appears in the document as an object, and the WordArt toolbar appears.

Click outside the object to deselect it.

Changing a WordArt text effect

In Normal or Slide view, activate the slide that contains the WordArt object.
Click the WordArt object to select it.

The WordArt toolbar appears.

ᗏ Use the buttons on the **WordArt** toolbar to make your changes.

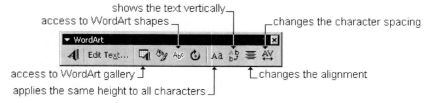

*The **Edit Text** button reopens the text editing dialog box.*

Inserting a WordArt object

The text is shown without the selected effect in the dialog box.

Changing a WordArt text effect

Click and drag the yellow diamond to change the angle of the WordArt object.

Freehand drawing

In Normal or Slide view, activate the slide concerned.

Open the **AutoShapes** list and point to **Lines**.

According to what sort of line you want to draw, click:

 to draw a series of curved lines.

 to draw a freeform shape made of curved and straight sections.

to draw as if with a pencil (PowerPoint calls this type of drawing a scribbles).

To draw a Curve, make successive mouse-clicks (the pointer is a black cross).

To draw a Freeform, make successive mouse-clicks for the straight sections, and drag for the curved sections (the pointer looks like a pencil).

To draw a Scribble, drag the pointer (it looks like a pencil).

Finish a **Curve** or **Freeform** by double-clicking the location of the last point (for an open shape), or near the start of the shape (for a closed, and coloured, shape).

To finish a **Scribble**, release the mouse button.

Freehand drawing

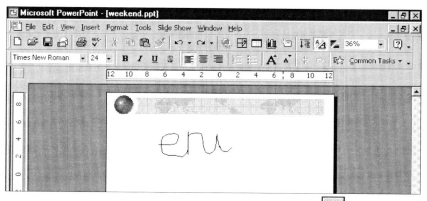

This drawing was made with the Scribble tool

PERSONAL NOTES

Chapter 7

OBJECTS

Deleting objects

Go to Normal or Slide view.

Activate the slide that contains the object you want to delete.

Select the object by clicking it.

If you want to delete several objects, select them using ⇧ Shift *-clicks.*

↳ **Edit - Clear** or Del

Resizing objects

Go to Normal or Slide view.

Activate the slide that contains the object you want to resize.

Select the object.

Format - Colors and Lines

Click the **Size** tab.

↳ Enter the new dimensions in the **Height** and **Width** boxes in the **Size and rotate** frame if you want to use centimetres as the unit or measurement. If you enter values in the **Height** and **Width** boxes in the **Scale** frame, you must use percentages.

Confirm with **OK**.

 You can resize an object using the mouse. Select it, point to one of the selection handles (the pointer takes the shape of a two-headed arrow) then drag.

Deleting objects

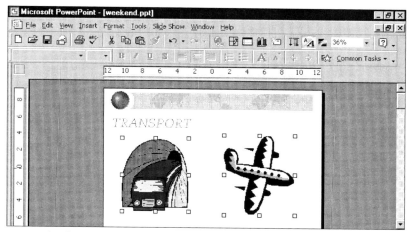

In this example, two objects have been selected to be deleted.

Resizing objects

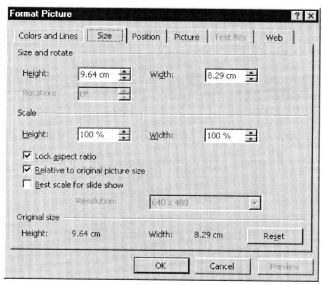

The **Lock aspect ratio** option allows you to keep the selected object's height and width in proportion.

Creating and using slide shows

Changing the orientation of an object

Go to Normal or Slide view.

Activate the slide that contains the object whose orientation you want to change.
Select this object.
Open the list on the **Draw** button on the **Drawing** toolbar.

> Click the **Rotate or Flip** option.
> Click one of the following:

Rotate Left	to rotate the selected object 90° to the left.
Rotate Right	to rotate the selected object 90° to the right.
Flip Horizontal	to turn the object horizontally through 180°.
Flip Vertical	to turn the object vertically through 180° (top to bottom).

You cannot change the orientation of some objects like pictures and OLE objects.

Rotating an object freely

Go to Normal or Slide view.

Activate the slide that contains the object in question.
Select the object concerned.

Click the [⟳] button on the **Drawing** toolbar.
Point to one of the object's handles.

The mouse pointer takes on a similar shape to the [⟳] icon.

> Drag one of the handles in the direction you want to turn the object.

Click the [⟳] tool button again or press [Esc] to reselect the object.

*The [⟳] tool is the same as the **Format - Colors and Lines** command, Size tab, **Rotation** text box, or the **Rotate or Flip - Free Rotate** command in the **Draw** menu on the **Drawing** toolbar.*

Changing the orientation of an object

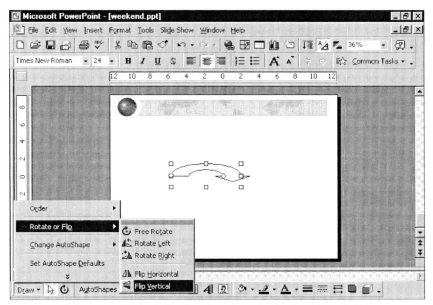

A drawing to the left of each option illustrates the rotation.

Rotating an object freely

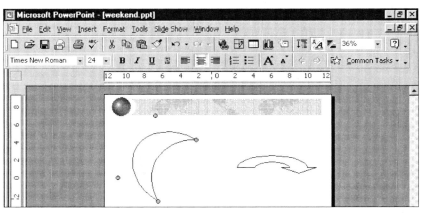

When you are rotating an object, the selection handles appear as green circles.

Creating and using slide shows

Aligning objects in relation to each other

In Slide or Normal view, activate the slide that contains the objects you want to align. Select these objects.

Open the **Draw** list on the **Drawing** toolbar.
Choose **Align or Distribute**.

 Activate the **Relative to Slide** option if you want to align the objects in relation to the page, or leave it inactive to align the objects with each other.

If you need to, open the **Draw** list on the **Drawing** toolbar and activate the **Align or Distribute** option again.

The first three choices are for the horizontal alignment and the next three for vertical alignment.

Click the alignment you want.

Changing the stacking order of objects

In Normal or Slide view, activate the slide in question and select the object concerned.

Open the **Draw** list on the **Drawing** toolbar.

Point to the **Order** option.

 Choose one of the following:

Bring to Front	place the selected object in front of all the others.
Send to Back	place the selected object behind all the others.
Bring Forward	move the selected object in front of the object immediately above it in the pile.
Send Backward	move the selected object behind the object immediately below it in the pile.

By default, objects are stacked in the order in which they were created or moved into the pile (the most recent are on top).

Microsoft PowerPoint 2000

Aligning objects in relation to each other

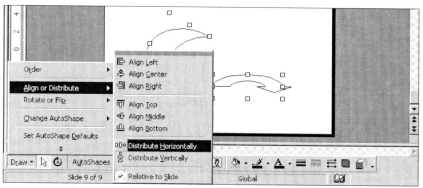

*A tick is shown to the left of the **Relative to Slide** option when it is active.*

Changing the stacking order of objects

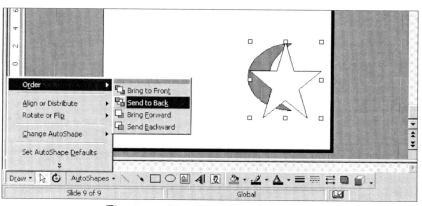

The star will be placed behind the moon.

Grouping objects

This technique is about grouping several objects so that you can work with them as though they were a single object (to move them all together, or apply the same fill colour, for example).

Activate the slide that contains the objects in question in Normal or Slide view.

Select the objects you want to group.

Open the **Draw** list on the **Drawing** toolbar.

 Click the **Group** or **Regroup** option.

*The **Regroup** option groups objects that were previously grouped, without you having to select them.*

A single selection frame appears around all the objects in the group.

Ungrouping objects

This technique separates grouped objects.

Activate the slide that contains the objects concerned in Normal or Slide view.

Select the objects you want to ungroup.

Open the **Draw** list on the **Drawing** toolbar.

Click **Ungroup**.

All the objects from the group are selected.

If you want to ungroup an object from the Clip Gallery, PowerPoint displays a message asking you for confirmation. Click **Yes** to ungroup the object or **No** if you do not want to.

Managing objects

Grouping objects

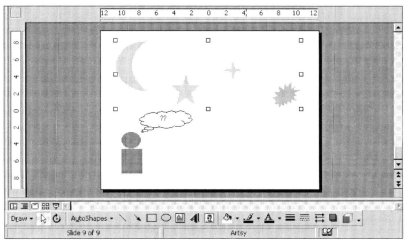

A single selection frame encloses the grouped objects:
they behave like one object.

Ungrouping objects

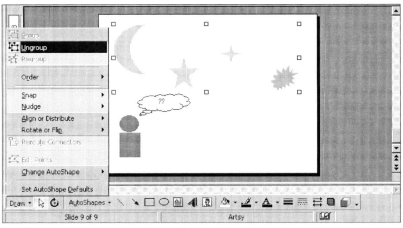

*The **Ungroup** option is only available if the objects have been grouped*
beforehand.

© Editions ENI - All rights reserved

Creating and using slide shows

153

Changing an object's borders

In Normal or Slide view, activate the slide that contains the object concerned.

Click in the object to select it. It might be a text box or a drawing created with the drawing tools.

Format - Colors and Lines

> Open the **Color** drop-down list in the **Line** frame and click one of the colours offered, or click **More Colors** and double-click the colour you want to use.
>
> Use the other options in the **Line** frame to define the appearance of the frame lines:
>
> | | |
> |---|---|
> | **Dashed** | to choose a dashed or continuous line. If you have chosen a patterned line, do not use these options. |
> | **Style** | to choose single or double lines, two lines with differing thickness, and so. |
> | **Weight** | to choose the thickness of the lines, in points. |
>
> Confirm these choices with **OK**.

> Titles, subtitles and bulleted lists are by default inserted in rectangular objects.

 You can also use the ▤ and ▤ buttons on the **Drawing** toolbar.

Changing an object's borders

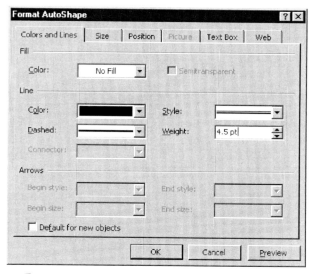

The **Connector** option is only available if the selected object is a connector line.

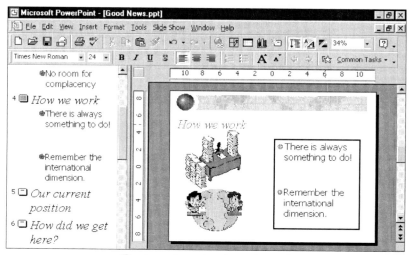

The text object has been framed.

Deleting an object's outline

Go to Normal or Slide view.

Activate the slide that contains the object in question.

Select the object whose outline you want to remove.

Open the list on the ![tool] tool on the **Drawing** toolbar by clicking the black triangle.

↳ Click the **No Line** option.

Applying a coloured fill to an object

Go to Normal or Slide view.

Activate the slide that contains the object in question.

Select the object whose fill you want to colour or recolour.

On the **Drawing** toolbar, open the list on the ![tool] tool by clicking the black triangle.

↳ If the colour you want to use is in the basic colour list, click it. If not, click **More Fill Colors** and double-click the colour you want to use.

Deleting an object's outline

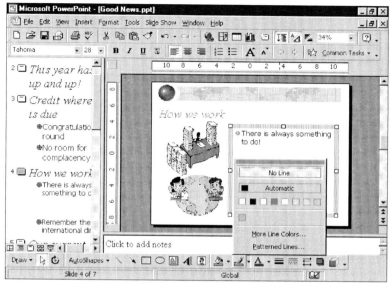

*The **Automatic** option applies the default frame colour from the active presentation's colour scheme.*

Applying a coloured fill to an object

*The **No Fill** choice can be used to remove the object's current fill.*

Creating and using slide shows

Using a texture as an object fill

Go to Normal or Slide view.

Activate the slide that contains the object that is to have a texture as its fill.

Select the object in question.

Click the black triangle on the ⬛ tool on the **Drawing** toolbar to open the list.

Click the **Fill Effects** option and activate the **Texture** tab.

> Select the texture you want to use.
>
> Confirm your choice by clicking **OK**.

Filling an object with a gradient

Go to Normal or Slide view.

Activate the slide in question.

Select the object that is to have a gradient.

Open the ⬛ list on the **Drawing** toolbar by clicking the black triangle.

Click the **Fill Effects** option and activate the **Gradient** tab.

> If you only want one colour in the gradient, activate **One color**, choose the colour from the **Color 1** list and drag the cursor towards **Dark** or **Light**.
>
> If you want to use two colours in the gradient, click **Two colors** and choose **Color 1** and **Color 2**.
>
> If you want to use several colours in the gradient, activate **Preset** and choose the effect you want in the **Preset colors** list.
>
> Whichever gradient you have selected, choose the **Shading styles** and click one of the **Variants** that are offered.
>
> Click **OK** to confirm these choices.

Using a texture as an object fill

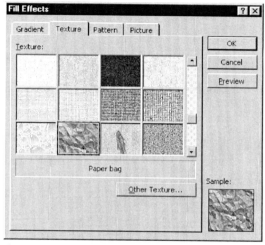

The name of the texture is written and a preview
is visible in the **Sample** frame.

Filling an object with a gradient

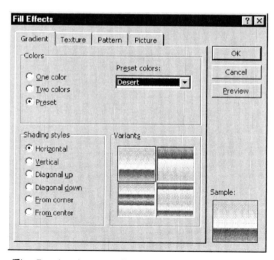

The **Preview** button allows you to apply the chosen
gradient to the selection without closing the dialog box.

Creating and using slide shows

Choosing a pattern for an object's fill

In Normal or Slide view, activate the slide concerned.

Select the object to which you want to apply a pattern.

Open the ▨ list on the **Drawing** toolbar by clicking the black triangle.

Click the **Fill Effects** option and activate the **Patterns** tab.

> Select the pattern you want to use.
>
> If you need to, choose the **Foreground** and **Background** colours.
>
> Confirm with **OK**.

Making a fill semitransparent

In Normal or Slide view, activate the slide concerned.

Select the object whose fill is to be made semitransparent.

Format - Colors and Lines

> Activate the **Semitransparent** option in the **Fill** frame.
>
> Click **OK** to confirm.

Choosing a pattern for an object's fill

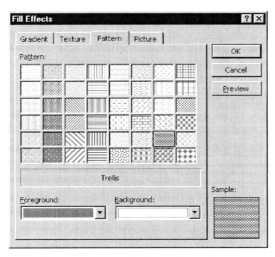

As soon as you select a pattern, its name
appears along with a sample.

Making a fill semitransparent

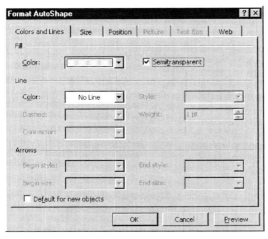

The *Semitransparent* choice is not available if the object
contains a gradient, pattern, texture or picture.

Inserting a picture as an object's fill

In Normal or Slide view, activate the slide concerned.

Select the object that is to have a picture as a fill.

Open the list on the **Drawing** toolbar by clicking the black triangle.

Choose the **Fill Effects** option and click the **Picture** tab.

Click **Select Picture**.

Choose the drive that contains the picture in the **Look in** drop-down list.

Go to the folder that contains the picture and open it by double-clicking its icon (yellow folder).

Select the picture file and click **Insert**, or simply double-click the picture's icon.

↳ Confirm by clicking **OK**.

Applying a 3-D effect to an object

In Normal or Slide view, go to the slide in question.

Select the object you want to show in 3-D.

Click the button on the **Drawing** toolbar.

↳ Click the 3-D effect you want to use.

A 3-D effect can only be applied to an object with a fill.

*The **3-D Settings** option allows you to customise the 3-D effect applied to the selected object.*

Inserting a picture as an object's fill

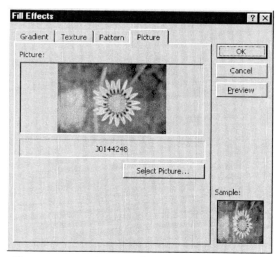

The picture is shown with its name and a sample.

Applying a 3-D effect to an object

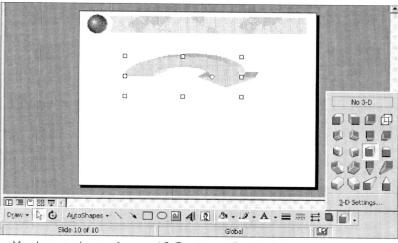

You have a choice of several 3-D effects. The No 3-D option transforms
a 3-D object into a two-dimensional one.

Creating and using slide shows

Applying a shadow to an object

You can add depth to an object by applying a shadow effect.

In Normal or Slide view, activate the slide concerned.

Select the object that is to have a shadow.

Click the button on the **Drawing** toolbar.
The No Shadow option removes any shadow effect.

ᗺ Click the shadow you want to apply.

*The **Shadow Settings** choice allows you to move the shadow, or apply a colour.*

You can use this tool to apply a shadow to an object and the text it contains.

Changing the appearance of arrowheads

In Normal or Slide view, activate the slide in question.

Select the arrow(s) you want to change.

Click the ⇄ button on the **Drawing** toolbar.

Select the option you want, or click **More Arrows**.
*This last option opens the **Format AutoShape** dialog box, **Colors and Lines** tab.*

ᗺ If you have chosen **More Arrows**, use the different lists in the **Arrows** frame to define the appearance at one end of the arrow (**Begin style, Begin size**), and at the other end (**End style, End size**).

Confirm with **OK**.

Applying a shadow to an object

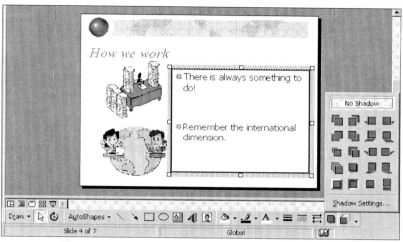

The object which is to have a shadow must have a fill.

Changing the appearance of arrowheads

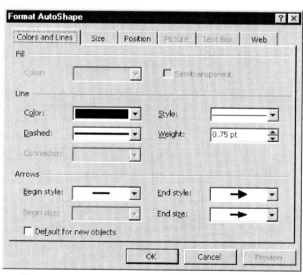

The **Preview** button allows to you to see the effect
on the object without closing the dialog box.

PERSONAL NOTES

_____

_____

_____

_____

_____

_____

_____

_____

_____

_____

_____

_____

_____

_____

_____

_____

_____

_____

_____

_____

_____

_____

_____

_____

_____

_____

_____

_____

_____

_____

Moving around in text

← / →	One character to the left/right
↑ ↓	One line up/down
Ctrl ← / Ctrl →	One word to the left/right
End / Home	To the end/beginning of a line
Ctrl ↑ / Ctrl ↓	One paragraph up/down
Ctrl End / Ctrl Home	To the end/begining of a text box
Ctrl Enter	To the next title or body text placeholder
⇧ Shift F4	Repeat the last Find action

Deleting text

← / Ctrl ←	Delete one character/word to the left
Del / Ctrl Del	Delete one character/word to the right

Selecting text and objects

⇧ Shift → / ⇧ Shift ←	One character to the right/left
Ctrl ⇧ Shift → / Ctrl ⇧ Shift ←	One word to the right/left
⇧ Shift ↑ / ⇧ Shift ↓	One line up/down
Esc	An object (with selected text inside the object)
⇄ or ⇧ Shift ⇄	An object (with an object selected)
Enter	Text within an object
Ctrl A (in the slide pane)	All objects
Ctrl A (in Slide sorter view)	All slides
Ctrl A (in the outline pane)	All text

Slide Show

N/`Enter`/`Pg Dn`
(or click the mouse)   Next animation or next slide
P/`Pg Up`   Previous animation or slide
"number" + `Enter`   Go to slide "number"
B or full-stop   Display a black screen
W or comma   Display a white screen
S or plus sign (+)   Stop or restart an automatic slide show
`Esc`   End a slide show
E   Erase on-screen annotations
H   Go to next hidden slide
T   Set new timings
O   Use original timings
M   Use mouse-click to advance
`Ctrl` **P**   Change the pointer to a pen
`Ctrl` **A**   Change the pointer to an arrow
`Ctrl` **H**   Hide the pointer and button immediately
`Ctrl` **U**   Hide the pointer and button in 15 seconds
`⇧ Shift` `F10`   Display the shortcut menu
`⇄`/`⇧ Shift` `⇄`   Go to the next/previous hyperlink

Working in an outline

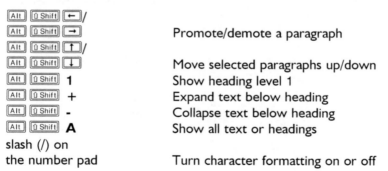

`Alt` `⇧ Shift` `←`/
`Alt` `⇧ Shift` `→`   Promote/demote a paragraph

`Alt` `⇧ Shift` `↑`/
`Alt` `⇧ Shift` `↓`   Move selected paragraphs up/down
`Alt` `⇧ Shift` **1**   Show heading level 1
`Alt` `⇧ Shift` **+**   Expand text below heading
`Alt` `⇧ Shift` **-**   Collapse text below heading
`Alt` `⇧ Shift` **A**   Show all text or headings
slash (/) on
the number pad   Turn character formatting on or off

Miscellaneous shortcut keys

| ⇧ Shift F10 | Display a shortcut menu |
| Alt space | Display the application's Control menu |

Menu shortcut keys

File

Ctrl N	New
Ctrl O	Open
Ctrl S	Save
Ctrl P	Print
Alt F4	Exit
Ctrl W	Close

Edit

Ctrl Z	Undo
Ctrl Y	Repeat
Ctrl X	Cut
Ctrl C	Copy
Ctrl V	Paste
Del	Clear
Ctrl ⇧ Shift C	Copy formats
Ctrl ⇧ Shift V	Paste formats
Ctrl A	Select all
Ctrl D	Duplicate
Ctrl F	Find
Ctrl H	Replace

View

| F5 | Run slide show |

Insert

| Ctrl M | New slide |
| Ctrl K | Hyperlink |

Format

`Ctrl` `⇧ Shift` **F**	Font
`Ctrl` **B**	Bold
`Ctrl` **I**	Italics
`Ctrl` **U**	Underline
`Ctrl` `⇧ Shift` **P**	Font size
`Ctrl` **+**	Subscript
`Ctrl` `⇧ Shift` **=**	Superscript
`Ctrl` `space`	Remove formatting

Alignment

`Ctrl` **L**	Left
`Ctrl` **E**	Center
`Ctrl` **R**	Right
`Ctrl` **J**	Justify
`⇧ Shift` `F3`	Change the case

Tools

`F7`	Spelling

Macro

`Alt` `F8`	Macros
`Alt` `F11`	Visual Basic Editor

Window

`F6`	Next pane
`⇧ Shift` `F6`	Previous pane

Help

`F1`	Microsoft PowerPoint help
`⇧ Shift` `F1`	What's this?

Microsoft PowerPoint 2000

INDEX BY SUBJECT

▲ Quick Reference Guide ▲ Practical Guide ▲ Microsoft® Approved
▲ User Manual ▲ Training CD-ROM Publication

VISIT OUR WEB SITE http://www.editions-eni.com

Ask for
our free brochure

**For more information
on our new titles
please complete
this card and return**

Name: ....

....

Company: ....

Address: ....

....

Postcode: ....

Town: ....

Phone: ....

E-mail: ....

ENI Publishing LTD

500 Chiswick High Road

London W4 5RG

THE WORKS

PUBLISHERS
PRICE.

£7.99
NOW ONLY

£1.99

BIG SAVINGS !

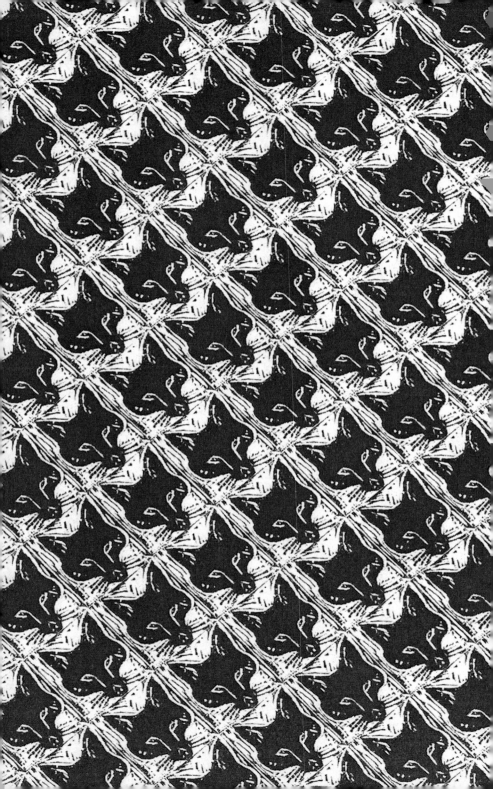

Riding The Tears Of Everest

By
Darren Clarkson

Published by Urban Fox Press
urbanfoxpress@hotmail.com
www.urbanfoxpress.ik.com

First published 2005

Printed in Kent, England

ISBN 0-9547374-8-2

Riding The Tears Of Everest

"Sagamartha Cries"

By
Darren Clarkson

Darren Clarkson, or Daz to those who know him, was born in 1975. As a child he grew up in the Britain that Thatcher inhabited, playing and learning only a stone throw from the crumbling Yorkshire coalfields.

Daz has been kayaking since his early teenage years and now takes to the water with every spare moment. After spending time at University he felt the need to travel and avoid getting a real job. He has spent many months spread over many years in Nepal kayaking the rivers and drinking coffee in Kathmandu. He has also dragged his boat to Pakistan, Morocco, France, Italy, Switzerland, Norway and Canada, along the way meeting the many good friends and interesting faces that will keep the fire burning in the belly for years to come.

For my parents
For the family
For all that want the dream to come true
For those that never made the last river
For those that we miss every hour of the day

Introduction

Running rivers in small plastic kayaks is a risky sport. It is not the basic messing about in boats of romantic ideals. And venturing to the highest point on the planet just to partake of such folly is seemingly foolhardy. Yet a small group of British travellers did just that.

Influenced by Lord Buddha, ethics, self-modesty and responsibility they floated towards India changed forever. What you are about to read is a brief account of the trip, a trip that changed the attitudes of the men forever.

The words have been pieced together from the obscure mindset of the author following on from the expedition. Many have called this mindset post-expedition trauma, an area significant to the individual and the group but often totally irrelevant to the larger audience and the reader. Let us hope this is not the case this time around.

The documenting of events is as close to the fact as the author can remember. Other words, principally those in *italic script,* are direct observations from the notes and diary made during the trip. Upon first reading the early chapters many may wonder when the white water action will happen. But persevere and although confusing and complex the story of the expedition will develop. This is not a river guidebook. It is a book of a journey.

1
Landing

...And so it was that the rain came thundering down the valley, like the riders of the apocalypse. Destruction flooded in the wake. On the last horse was death venturing forth with wrath to conquer the immortal soul of the impersonal culture. A culture that had evolved, spawned by the late 20th and early 21st century. The wonder of modern science had failed the masses. The populace dreamed of a 'New Hope'. A new guru was needed to lead them forward to the Shangri La that had been promised with the birth of the solitary Christ years before. Selfish was the culture; selfish was the individual.

It had been a long time since the people had possessed the same dream, the same goal. The collective conscious held little passion for this ideal. Stumbling blindly was not productive. It did not draw the much-needed conclusions. Moving the years from the pagan Norse gods to the collapse of the dollar worship of capital ideals, many idols have come and gone; many born and died. All were able to fool those who blinked, willing to listen. Firstly popular spiritual idols were found to fault, then the dominant ideology keep those of the populace separated at a fair distance. The self worked within the group as independence was neglected. From hoaxes to magicians, those who looked for escape could only dream a vain hope of finding a cure.

In the middle of Asia, sandwiched between the giant nations of China and India, I find myself with dust on my feet and a mind full of confusion. Confusion that is only balanced by wandering, walking. Every one wanders but many just take strolls allowing the mind to blue sky think. To escape in the mind to other places. I just know that once the dream is formed in my mind, once the seed of travel is planted, I have to act.

Only my sandals offer minimal protection from the grime of

the unkempt Himalayan roads criss-crossing Nepal. My hair, growing erratically with no particular style, is filthy whilst my cheeks itch with the bristles of a dishevelled beard. I've washed this morning but walking into the street makes me dirty again only seconds later. Sweat beads on my brow and my throat is sore from breathing the thick polluted air trapped in the Kathmandu Valley. It's an eco-community of global warming within the living green house formed due to the unique landscape.

Dressed in stereotypical traveller clothes, the uniform of the non-conformist, my thin cotton pants cling to my legs when gusts of wind whip up into a frenzy, flashing rubbish into vortexes around me. My shirt holds a thousand stains from sweat to curry to tea and soap. The shirt's colour, the colour it was in the shop, has long since gone, long since faded. Around my neck an old piece of string holds an emblem of the Lord Buddha cast in ceramic and looking tired and woeful. It is covered in a thin film, months worth of scum. Its one of those paradoxes of none attachment Buddhism. To buy something that represents the ideals so that you have a personal motto, a mantra around the body. I should have perhaps seen a conundrum just in this single item.

Attachment to the object that represents Buddha, becomes in this form a false idol, a (missed) representation to the masses of the instigator of the religion. Siddhartha, the man was a prince not a god. He is the self-proclaimed 'enlightened' being. Unlike Hindu gods or the effigies of Christ and Mary, Buddhism requires none attachment. Only when the *objet a* as the French call it, the vision of desire, is accepted as gone can the slightest hint of attachment, human nature, accept the possibilities of 'nothingness' of enlightenment.

External stimuli, that of the world outside the mind, is simple fantasy, a simple projection. It clouds the spirit. Nothing is real. The computer that I write this on, the book that it is in and the cause and effects of the daily grind simply prove to avoid the conflict of the internal ghost in the machine. So strong is the fantasy of daily life that western culture makes that its goal, makes it seem important. This is not to say that it isn't important. It's quite simple. Our internal view, the ghost, is barred, blocked by the external. Philosophers from Descartes to Kant have tried to understand the implications, and it is perhaps through reading such academic work that has influenced my thoughts on life.

Through these lonesome journeys deep in the Himalayas my mind ventures off at tangents. It is important to feel confused by these thoughts. It acts to underline the feelings and drive that I feel. How many times does the single human feel empathy with the surrounding area? Just because it is cold outside why does that instigate a feeling of 'the blues'? When the sun shines why do you feel happy? Its seems a psychosomatic dilution. So it's the questioning of these worldviews, and the reflection, that urges me into the situation. Urges me to question what I have been told to be real, that is accepted as the social process.

Armed military police flank the street by the embassy near the flat I live in. I walk past them daily on my stroll into the 'Drift Nepal' office. 'Drift Nepal' is a company full of local guides and old friends. A premier Raft outfitter running commercial rips for fee-paying adventure tourists in Nepal.

Police and army guard the city of Kathmandu. Guns are held in a haphazard manner, no doubt without bullets. It's no discredit but Nepal is one of the world's poorest countries, if not the poorest. These sort of statistics are banded around often. Bangladesh also has its fair share of published poverty, as too does Ethiopia and Sudan. It always seems a little strange to me to publish such details. It's akin to a school headmaster pointing out the least educated or poorest pupils for the ridicule of all.

In the streets of Kathmandu bullets are a luxury a government like this can ill afford. The threat that the guns might have bullets is often enough to keep the 'peace' for the most part. Although even this is becoming of elementary effectiveness. Nepal has a minimal concern for human rights and even less concern for this position on the world stage. The country is still trying hard to develop from the doldrums of society.

2
Habit To Cure

So they pray. The country is as desperate as the hobo on the edge of sanity, much like the man who has lost it all. Thoughts come and go, from the cardboard city to the drunk asleep on the park bench. A heaven must exist in some form for many have spent their time here on this Earth in a living nightmare like hell.

Cars pass me as I walk. The shrill of the horn never leaves Kathmandu. Vehicles overloaded with the strain of constant abuse stop without reason and drive without concern for other road users or their occupants. The carriageway hosts all sorts of macabre transport systems from the brightly painted Tata buses decorated with stencils of Ganesh and Krishna to pedal driven rickshaws, a hybrid bicycle and cart for people and cargo. Then there's the porters carrying many kilos from tables to foodstuffs on their backs.

"Taxi,Taxi," the tired face of the driver hangs out of the window of a battered Suzuki mini-van. His hair is dark black and greasy, he carries an air of sleaze. Distorted speakers, cracked and wired badly echo with the vibrations of Asha Boslie. The shrill voice of the Bollywood singer holds the anguish of courtly love, in keeping with the tradition for the arrangement of marriage.

"Hello sir, you want taxi...your price, where you go," then he leans over and opens the back door to beckon me inside. Walking on without the slightest notice of the mayhem or the sales patter of this small business tycoon has become a daily chore. I've spent too many hours in these back lanes, in these overcrowded streets to be taken for a tourist. These streets are like home. I have a greater knowledge of Kathmandu than my own hometown. I'm not a city person. I hate the hustle and the noise, but somehow Kathmandu is different. For reasons I cannot explain I'm drawn here year after year. It's a habit that

I don't want to break. Perhaps it's the same thought process that smokers have when they know they should give up but the actual act gives so much pleasure.

Kathmandu is busy with the hordes of tourists mixing with the locals and the refugees. It's the fall season of 2003, October, and exteriors of happiness are resonated on the faces of the citizens. Joy and pleasure, the result of marketable spin, are produced by the history and the expectations of those who visit.

Like the masks in the old market of Durbar Square the city is hiding from a true gaze. Ashamed of it's real face. Since the murder of the King by his son a few years ago a wicked underbelly is killing the place. The spirit of Nepal in general is dying. Unsettled doctrines are forcing people to think. It's a cancerous underground war that is being waged on the home front.

As I jump over the puddles in the pavement, basic cracks within the infrastructure, I'm jostled by school children of all ages. Dressed in blue they smile and share jokes, gossip and giggle, just like all other kids in the world. Its early morning and the smog blankets lifting from the streets allow no place for the dirt to hide. The city is not quite awake. Neither am I. A few yards down the road I stare blankly through greasy stained glass at the bored looking clerks who sit behind the empty desks at the 'Druk Air' office. The national airline for Bhutan obviously doesn't want to promote tourism to its country. The pen pushers with shirt and ties do little for promoting one of the last untamed kingdoms of the world. Perhaps they have seen the pollutant of tourist intervention on its neighbours, other Himalayan Kingdoms, and wants to preserve the last Shangri La for the true freedom of expression for its people.

Kerosene stoves on portable barrows sit stationary at the side of the road. The sweet smell of curry made by these street vendors invades the nostrils, tempting me. The cheeky dimpled smile and the bright faces warm me. At times the food tastes like a thousand angels dancing on the tongue but for the most part its just non-descript mush, a cheap fuel for the body. Rice, lentils and eggs the staple diets. Alas the everyday habit of challenging my constitution is getting a little thin. Part of me still aches for the trappings of the western world that seems so far away. Simple pleasures like drinking water from taps without thinking about the possibilities of catching some virus that would make me bed bound for days.

Walking deep into the tourist hub I try to look for a pleasant establishment to temp me and wake me up. The 'Himalaya Java' coffee shop frequented by the elite café society proves the ideal place for the caffeine kick I need. It is a modern building seemingly out of place in Nepal. Scooters are parked outside next to 4x4 cruisers for the overland diplomats. A table by the door holds the helmets and briefcases that accompany such travel. Well-to-do Nepalese youths answer mobiles and arrange to meet via text message. There is on air of sophistication and an ethos that echo's with the resonance of coffee shops around the world. I sit alone in the corner of the roof terrace, sipping at a café latte and eating a cinnamon roll. All it takes now is for a group of twentysomethings to discuss relationships as they sit on the sofa next to me. Should this happen? I will know for sure that Nepal has cast off its roots of enlightenment? Welcome to Eastern sitcom land.

Many frequent visitor's to Kathmandu, as well as locals, have noted how Kathmandu is rushing headlong into the consumer age. With a shopping mall, the old city of the hippie route has all the joys and trappings of consumerism gone mad. Like the Hells Angels offering security at post 'Woodstock' concerts that proved the death of the flower power generation. The hippie trail is warped. Dying like the week old flowers on my window, the ones I forgot to water and didn't nurture.

Roaming the streets daily I have become seduced by the laptops and the mobile phones. The 'Nike' shop in the upmarket building just opposite the Royal Palace finds Buddhist monks in saffron robes trying on trainers. It's not just the shops that have jumped too fast into Western styles. In the nightclubs of Thamel the tourist district pimps parade girls of the night for the delight of both Indian and Western customers. These girls are dressed in what is supposed to be the latest Westerns styles, Kappa hats, Tracksuits, Diesel jeans and Calvin's (the true CK's). In Britain these kids would have Giros burning holes into the fabric of the shell suits.

Working girls and boys sit alone on stained sofas in dimly lit recesses of the slime ridden nightclubs. Like mermaids for drunken sailors the flicking fluorescent lights pull, drawing the unsuspecting pray, who crash on the rocks below. Just before the kill, muscle men step in and request payment. How many have fallen prey to the charms of them? Too drunk or stoned to care. Only with the cold light of day do they realise the error, the lady-boy sales commodity, where everything in Nepal can be bought for a price? Love you long-time, ten-dollar…

But it's worse just than that. Stories of sexual assaults on lone women travellers are ripe. The days are fading when women from the West were treated with respect like royalty. Street fights and bar brawls are now a common place in the cold night, as bars become ever eager to ask customers to loose rupees on imported spirits. Broken bottles line the beer stained floor of the vast amount of bars that have become part of the fabric of the tourist arena. Those worse for the intoxication stand in the corner of the room whilst vomiting on the floor. Overland tour groups meet and copulate in the back alley behind the 24hr sandwich shop next to the rubbish bins. This is the scene of how a civilised society lives. It is the place that represents the western world in this region of the high Himalayas.

As I sit in these times of conflict I wonder if the representation of the modern lifestyle is the aim? An emulation of 'western' cultural setting that is promoted as the goal! It reminds me of the stories about the influence of television on the masses. With the impending collapse it brings. Bhutan, the isolated neighbour of Nepal, has only in the last few years offered televisions to its people. The channels depict programs from the UK and America. How far they are from the culture of Bhutan. What reference do they have? Its been documented that the arrival of the small screen to this land is also the arrival of corruption, of crime and dishonesty. Bhutan now has a drug problem. It has homicide and depravity.

So it begs me to think. Have we, the modern West, brought this poison on the world?

3
Villains And Lies

Enlightenment often comes from the mouths of fools. The gurus are wearing Nike. The gods no longer rule the kingdom. Violence and destruction are at home here now. Morals decay whilst all the eggs in the basket are cracked.

Such is the way of the world, the need to explore and the secret that is locked behind closed doors at border posts. Visa checks and passport stamps are just another form of collection. Like putting stickers on your suitcase to show the world where you've been.

Many years of insurrection have meant that the underground resistance to the political ideology has lead to strikes. This is just the common face of the seemingly wanton decay. These cause havoc to the economics of Nepal, and to Kathmandu in particular. Tourists and the marketable union they bring become hostages in hotels just because they cannot get around town.

Issues from rising taxes to ethics and human rights become the catalysts for these displays of discontent. Throughout the strikes, commonly known as 'bandhs', shops are closed and taxis do not run for fear of becoming ambushed for breaking the strike. News is often ripe of the strike instigators petrol bombing those who, to coin a phrase from the mining conflict in Britain in the 1980s, become scabs. The bandh becomes a psychological mind war with the populace. Messages were beginning to be taken seriously by the government. I imagined a conversation with Diwalker Chand, author of 'Nepal's Tourism: Uncensored Facts', as I read his book.

"Imagine the tourist arriving on strike day!" In the confusion of my daydream I could hear the nervous quiver in his voice. "With no traffic allowed how could they leave the airport? Would they be forced to walk the empty street looking for shelter? Even on a normal day the transporting of tourists to the hotels is chaotic. The Maoist cause is felt directly by everyone from visitors to foreigners. It shows the malcontent of a culture that is changing."

Through every sip of coffee I wonder what happened to the Kingdom where Hindu and Buddhist beliefs run side by side. Even though I'm still here, still on my own quest, the interpretation of the Sanskrit is beckoning to the Western mind. Perhaps the reason that I'm so philosophical of late is that these streets add a particular normality to my life. Having just returned from a kayaking trip that made me question my own values, my own attitude to life.

It wasn't a normal trip for me, it was the cultivation of a dream, of a hope, that had started 18 months previously.

The arguments kept coming. Soaps operas flickered on the television retelling the tales of lost loves and broken homes. Colour swatches for interior décor held little significance. Whilst the constant barrage of advertising cut deep the gaze of the outside world forever. It dominated the home. A cry for freedom from the trappings of an ill matched relationship, a joint human affair.

I'd just planned to take part in a kayaking trip to the Upper Arun gorges in Nepal, due to set off in the spring of 2002. For many this region was known as the dark side of Everest. It is based around a river older than the great mountain. The river Arun existed before the Everest massif and with the shift of the Earth's crust the mountains grew at either side causing the river to become entrenched in a deep gorge.

The river Arun is one of the few secret rivers in Nepal, a gorge that rarely tempts kayakers and explorers. So important was the journey that I produced many an article for magazine and Internet web sites. The general consciences for the adventure was wide and ill informed at times but it proved to be the jump platform for what was needed to plant the seed for future games for further adventurers.

As one-trip closes the page is turned and the chapter starts for a new adventure. As I submitted the words below to print my mind wandered to future games. Just reading them in the British paddle sport magazine takes me back to that time...

It will soon be the time of year again when the monsoon rains halt in the river paradise of Nepal and commercial raft trips, river running and trekking groups embark on the Himalayan kingdom of Nepal. Those that are planning a trip out to the country this coming season this tale of caution from the spring 2002 March/April session may raise doubt or full further exploits. Our goal in this instance was to walk into the Arun valley, between Everest and Makalu, before venturing down the mighty Arun river. We were self supported and via the help of porters carried all our boats and kit for 6 days towards the river.

"What are you doing here?" The broken English of a Nepali youth questioned our presence in the small trade route village of Num. He continued, '"you cannot be here," or words to that effect. As smoke from the open fire filled the room we sat waiting, interrogated by this youth and his friends. It become apparent, things were not going to be as easy as normal. These guys would not fall for a quick feel of our boats and a bit of Basic English Teaching.

More so, this situation was tense, unlike normal Nepali greetings. Something was wrong, most defiantly wrong. After heated debates it became clear we were not in the presence of 'normal village residents'. More accurately we were in a Maoist strong hold. These guys were, for all intents and purposes, terrorists. We had heard the stories and read the papers before our departure from the UK, but we never expected to meet these people.

Their aim it seems is to destroy the infrastructure of an already suffering country. After our meeting they proceeded in destroying water stations power plants, schools, buses, airports and police stations, all for the sake of progress. If only I had known, perhaps I wouldn't have told him to go forth and multiply.

Now I have said these words before to those that get under my skin, and I must be a scary Yorkshire bloke as they tend to back off, but these were different. They were quite persistent. It was looking more and more like we were under 'house arrest' and that the river Arun, our goal, would be out of reach.

Was the river going to beat us before we had even put on our boating kit? We doubted it. We had not walked for 6 days towards Makalu to paddle the river, one of the most powerful in the Himalayas that takes water from Everest and Makalu among others, only to be scared by the rebels!

At 4.45 the following morning we slipped out of the village, not waiting to discuss our plans with the Maoist leaders. By 9.00 we had seen the sunrise over the giant Himalayan peaks and were well on our way down the Arun Gorges (left unpadded for about 8 years). This day was a wake up call for the rest of the trip. Before lunch we had encountered our first portage. Crossing from bank to bank we tried to fathom an escape route up the gorge walls.

Upon approaching the river's right bank we came across an almost vertical rock face. Portages would be tricky, even after a rope-assisted climb. So again we ferried over the river, to the river left and proceed to trek through the jungle. After sneaking the first class 6 later that day we pulled onto a white sandy beach to sleep for the night. Then it happened, a storm was brewing, thunder and lightening came violently up the gorge. The rains came unabated, having no respect for the 'dry season'. Perhaps the monsoon had arrived 4 weeks early?

Craig, who a few years earlier had paddled the 'other river of Everest', summarised day two as we huddled in a cave away from the rain. With a whit and style that would make Noel Coward run for the hills he remarked

"Yesterday I spent the day doing what I most love in the world, running hard whitewater with good friends.'

"And today Craig, what about today?"

"Well today, I did what I second most love doing in the world, portaging even harder water with good friends,'

Now day 3, well this was gonna shake things up a bit. But what to do? We were committed, early on in the day, just after breakfast and a miss timed move. An incorrect line saw me doing ten rounds with the 10-15 foot tow back of a small bungalow pour-over. This maelstrom of whitewater had a power that I had never experienced before in all my years of river running. The river god was not happy with me or my plans of escape. Water filled my lungs as I was twisted and tussled violently by this river. Needless to say I jettisoned my boat and made a swim for freedom. Open to eventual rescue I coughed up a lot of water, my head was spinning and my gear was ripped. My life-jacket and waterproof trousers showed the abrasion. It was a long haul in difficult water, swimming for a longer distance than we'd actually paddled the previous day!

The rest of the day saw no swims and some brilliant high-class water. As the rains came again during the night sanity became thought provoking.

"Marriage and kids must be easier than this shit." Voicing these thoughts to the others I estimated we only have 3 or 4 more river days left. We just hoped that the food would hold out.

By the 30 March we had made it to Bumlingtar. The gorge walls had started to open up, people we visible on the banks, the last class 5+ was behind us. With relief we disembarked early to rest for the night, our thoughts were now centred on getting to the confluence with the Sun Kosi. We were unsure if the Maoist would be following our progress as during the day we had heard gunfire. We needed to feel secure again. Perhaps the often travel Sun Kosi/Sapta Kosi would offer such assurance.

The following day was our last full day on the river although we didn't know it. On the night of the 31 March the rains came, faster than they had previously, so hard, so fast, that even the gore-tex of our bivvy bags could not cope. Upon waking the river has risen about 4ft and turned a chocolate brown, silt, wood, rubbish, dead things all flowed down, hence forth to the Bay of Bengal. This was Hepatitis country and my jabs weren't up to date. We had estimated that from setting off on the 1ˢᵗ April we would perhaps have 2 days left on the river. How wrong we were, with the increase in water we were not gonna be slow. By lunchtime we had made it to the Sun Kosi and were sitting at Tribani with lunch and a feeling of joy in our bellies. It then dawned on us... The Sun Kosi, the major river, actually had less volume that the Arun, one of its tributaries. Boy that was strange. Perhaps the river gods had tried to fox us and sent the rains only to our gorge. It seemed that way.

Before our muscles ceased we set forth into the Sun Kosi/Sapta Kosi. The take out was at Chatra, we had made it, success. This was no time to relax though, as a dead body floated past in the stream. The remnants of a previous funeral pyre...

Upon disembarking in Chatra we headed for a bus back to the capital, Kathmandu only to be informed that due to Maoist presence in the area a national strike had been called. We would have to wait in this 'arm pit of the world' for a week.

"Not a chance," said Rob, as we hired a ex-British Landrover with suspect brakes to race across the Terai so that we could jump a bus that was supposed to be leaving for the 14 hour ride back Kathmandu.

After strapping the boats to the bus we were intellectually informed that only 1 seat was available, but we had no choice as we snuggled on to the back seat. This bench seat was a sight, with vomiting kids, fat Indians and 3 tired and scruffy British kayakers still in river kit. This bus trip was 14 hours of paradise, who had the Valium?

4
Crumbs On The Carpet

However, quick recollections fade into the night as emotions are tied to the heart. What has once been for better and worse now situates with worse. A devil lies. A discussion made matters worse. The wrong and right, the path, open crossroads, just await. The choices a greater part who try to effect life.

After putting down the flimsy English language 'Rising Nepal' newspaper I root into my oversized shoulder bag for my wallet, pencil and diary. With each turn of the diary page the scribble reads of what I have accomplished, what has become, and what will be in the future. The writing tiny and squashed onto the paper is difficult even for me to understand. A library would have provided the quiet for such scholarly work. All I have is the modern comfort of the coffee shop. How much is difficult to read seems strange since it is my hand that imprinted it. With a free flow lack of consciousness script littered with broken syntax.

Choosing the path of the explorer seems a selfish indulgence. It is a route of all evil and the fault of the lifestyle choice. This expedition to Nepal came from behind, crawling up on me somewhat unexpected. I had taken a gap year many years ago and thought I had settled but the Dudh Kosi proved to be an escape. It was a focus. It was all I had after the years within a failed relationship. I knew something else must exist. If someone else were to tell the story of why I did the Dudh Kosi they would no doubt say it was either a cry for help, a route to escape or a suicide bid. Why else would a sane person pit themselves against a ranging torrent where death could come at any time? I didn't know how true any of that was but I know I wasn't myself.

After the breakdown of the relationship I spent time living in my car finding myself as a social outcast. True, I had a job and my parents put me up as I stored kit in the garage but I spend more nights in tents and sleeping rough than in a bed enclosed within four walls. I was a wreck. I had no self-esteem at all. All I wanted was to be accepted. Trying too hard, whilst not thinking of others. I insulted plenty of people, although I never meant to, and I lost a lot of friends. People who I thought were friends deserted me. Its no mistake that I felt I was drowning...out of my depth, out of air. Only months earlier I had been on anti-depressant tranquillisers to trim the overflow of a stress-related breakdown. I spoke honestly in the confused state. I didn't understand myself and I doubt others would care to help me back on the path to be socially accepted.

Prompted to act, the famous river of Everest the Dudh Kosi was turned into a site of pilgrimage. Two friends, perhaps the only ones I had left, held the same passion for the river that I had; they wanted to paddle down from Everest. They were with me to help me on a quest. Perhaps this sort of life changing route is missed in this world. It creeps up on you. It's a surprise.

Martyn, short and stout, is a concerned man. His hard exterior often makes him look angry. He had a liking for the ladies but this had stopped since he met the love of his life. Then there was Dave. A scruffier tramp would be hard to find, but he has a heart of gold and is full of contradictions. He is one of the best white water paddlers I know and is an inspiration. Through all his years kayaking in Nepal he has gained the 'nickname' Crazy Dave, although I know for sure that this isn't true. He has a true adventure spirit and people don't quite understand him and the risks he is willing to take for his bit of freedom. Then myself, a self-verifying disillusioned paranoid social inept Northerner. I enjoy solo boating and solo travel; I don't drink and don't smoke and yet I find myself in the dirtiest and smokiest bars in Asia with friends. That was the group for the Dudh Kosi. It would be the end, a chapter. For what is really left when you've paddled down both sides of Everest into the Himalayan Kingdom of Nepal? As I was set to do. I felt the weight on my shoulders. If success would come I assumed I would be the second living person ever to do the task.

17 Oct 03
It was a long flight, with delays and not enough sleep. Martyn insists I was dead to the world. I made the flight from London straight after a late night shift at work.

Dave was already in Kathmandu when Martyn and myself arrived off the plane from London. Like every night he was sat in a low-down dirty bar, tucked out of the way down a damp pathway opposite the French Embassy. A jazz bar owned by a friend of his that became a second home. Positioned within the upmarket Embassy district the bar was within crawling distance of the flat we shared. It was a common place to locate Dave. He was drinking from a bottle of red wine and although he had obviously been in the bar for most of the day he wasn't that drunk. Dave never really got drunk. I think his body was used to the abuse that he put it through. He could always remember and when things mattered he managed to pull out all the stops in order to get the job done.

We found him walking without his shoes around the bar, talking to everyone and anyone that would listen. Upon seeing us he was ecstatic, pleased to say the least. As our flight had been delayed he'd been waiting all day for us.

"Sit down lads," taking a seat on the floor Dave waved at the barman, "Kumar, get these boys a drink." Five minutes later a long haired Nepalese lad with the broadest smile and pearl white teeth brought Martyn a beer and Dave his usual triple Rum and Coke, in a pint pot, so he could drink it with the red wine he was holding at the time. Shortly after the alcoholic drinks had been brought over a half-pint cup of tea arrived for me. Then Kumar pulling his hair into a ponytail with a grubby elastic band returned to the bar. Flicking through a scattering of bootleg CD's he inserted yet another 'Jazz Compilation' with Dizzie Gillespie blearing out on his horn. The decrepit multi-stack stereo system struggled to cope.

In this company I'm quite glad I don't drink. They had been known to loose days due to drinking binges. But they were happy drunks for the most part. We sat in the dimly lit 'lounge' area of the bar as Dave told us about his news for our forth coming trip whilst drawing heavy on a local cigarette rolled tightly with four rolling papers. He waved his arms wildly and told how he had booked a small plane to fly us to Lukla. Ash clung flimsily to the end of the rolled paper cigarette. Dave not noticing placed it into his mouth again whilst a clump of ash fell to his chest. Brushing it aside his bearded smile told everyone how exited he was. We couldn't turn back, he'd paid the deposit and set a friend to work in the search for a group of porters. From the appearance of a low-down drunk he'd worked hard.

When I was back in England Dave had sent me an email saying that he'd arrived in Nepal and was busy getting drunk. From that email he had inspired no confidence and I doubted that the trip would work. But a light was certainly shining on us now. So we sat as Dave spoke rapidly about the trip. We were huddled together on the floor. Gathered around an old tyre made into a table. Joining us at the table was a girl, Nat', who had befriended Martyn and myself during a plane transfer in one of the Arab states. It was her first time in Nepal. Canadian by birth she had flown first to London before joining the flight we were on. I don't know what she made of this group of blokes she now found herself sat with. Even after all the air miles we had shared she somehow looked clean and un-creased. I felt dirty and knew that I would feel no cleaner whilst I was in this country.

18 Oct 04

Waking with a heavy head, drinking water from the taps...here it is yet another Nepal season. Would this one be different? Thinking from the events of last night that we are in well over our heads. This sort of trip is left for the expedition elite. How are we going to compere. We are not professional kayakers, skilled yes, but that's not in the same ballpark. Unlike other trips that class as major expeditions we are self-funding, begging and borrowing money. The only true sponsorship is from Corvedalecare, who I work for, who've offered a cash donation and time off. All our boats and kit have been purchased at discount from suppliers and friends.

Everest, the high dream for many a climber, from the brash Kiwi who pushed forward the perimeter of the British attempts, to the faces of those who had lost their way and fallen foul of the mountain, those who never made it down. It is not a route for the feint hearted. If it were easy then it would be of no conquest at all.

Climbers look up to the peak thinking of the Western Cwm and the advanced and technical Hillary step. Those with a passion of kayaking adventures scrutinise the mountain for the tears of the great goddess mother of the earth. Descents are few and far between on the great rivers.

The goddess, Everest, cries twice into Nepal. Both rivers are technically difficult and at the limit of the possible. The Arun drains from the backside of Everest, the Tibet side, whilst the Dudh Kosi drains from the dominant Nepal side. Both of these rivers are the tears of the Solu Khumbu and both hold the passion for a unique adventure. Many questions are raised. Is it for the modicum of fame that I must continue down river? Is it the bond that I have with friends? Do others care about the adventure? Should they? Is it because those with the trappings of modern living don't care that I should?

Even putting the pages together, putting on paper my experiences, I dwell thinking. At what cost is adventure?

Is it because that there are not many of 'us' left? Not many adventurers left? Not much left to qualify as adventure? How does the mind become fuelled with the quest and passion that adventure entails. It's the law of the nomad. Just too scared to go home for long. Its too much of a bounded system. Too much responsibility to not know the planet. Too much out in the wild and windless wonders to just sit and forge a life at home.

Falling from Everest the cascade of water that is the Dudh Kosi has seen seldom descents. None to our knowledge have ever been made on a complete descent from the Tributaries all the way to India, a descent encompassing the whole length of Nepal. Pioneers of expedition kayaking, a British team lead by Mike Jones, did accomplish a descent of plenty of the river in the 1970s but due to the logistics and the complexities of travel at the time only certain members of the trip paddled certain sections. It is true that the expedition made the descent but the 'paddlers', the individuals, didn't all do the whole navigable sections. They were pathfinders and inspirations for the growing number of expedition kayakers around the world who dreamed and lived only for exploring. The achievement they made far outweighs that of any subsequent attempts, ours included.

Those members of this first descent British expedition, still living, are pushing back the boundaries of expedition big water kayaking to this day. Other notable descents are for a group of British kayakers back in the late 1990s who had a minor epic when they had to walk out and had many portages to deal with. Having said that it is the members of this group that brought the Dudh Kosi back into the minds of paddlers around the world. Craig Dearing, one of the paddlers on this ill-fated trip, was also on the Arun gorges river trip with me.

It was the last major expedition on the Dudh Kosi that offered the most help. Gerry Moffat, a veteran kayaker based in Nepal for many years, was part of an international team that did the river from Jorselle just below Namche Bazaar, a few years previous. Gerry, an old drinking friend of Dave's, was a wealth of knowledge and gave us the benefit of his experience, prior to our departure. If you didn't know Gerry I doubt you could trust him. His face showed the ravages of time, his uncombed hair poked from beneath a strap cap visor as he ambled around the restaurants of Thamel. With one leg of his trousers pushed up to the calf whilst the other was rolled down. He constantly gave the impression that he had just got out of bed. He might just have had. Himalayan conquests were his forte. Kathmandu was one of those sorts of places, full of those that didn't quiet fit. The Dudh Kosi was worse, it acted like a magnet drawing souls ever nearer. If you'd done the Dudh then everyone in the rafting industry knew you. Often they branded you a fool and reckless. Rarely did they call you heroic or brave.

Only with the actual arrival in the Himalayas did the feeling of 'I'm putting the hold on my life back home and searching for this ideal' evolve. I tried every hour of the day to understand why we staked our lives for a bit of emancipation, to push back the past and put phantoms to rest.

It has been a long time coming. Prior to departing for the trip, knowing that, with a high possibility of death, life offers too many burnt bridges and broken rocks. It would perhaps be cathartic to mend the bridges and glue the rocks. So I started getting in touch with old friends and hoped a resolve with old problems would be liberating.

"Kate, hi it's me... Daz, we... 'er, lived together once."

"O, hi."

"Just wondered how you are and well what you been up to."

"Just trying to run a business with my partner."

"That sounds good, look I'm sorry for…well you know."

"It was a long time ago now."

"I don't want the bridge to be all gone, if off to Everest and I don't want to go knowing that…"

"It's all ok now, things have moved on, hope you have a good holiday."

Then she hung up. It was always the same.

Selfishness to compere myself to others. Past partners, previous relationships and violation, distrust, lies and broken memories are brought to mind. What might have been and what never was appear in conversation and fade into the night. Pointing to the many reasons of emancipation, a grasp away from those who follow blindly.

In the small hours of the late night as it fades into the early morning thoughts paralyse the mind. They take a hold on what should be kept private, what should be an inner demon. We all have reasons for coming to Nepal. All the backpackers 'gap' year students. All the middle market travellers and 'adventure' seekers huddle under this umbrella term. Some venture forth into this country with the promise of the mystic east to escape reality. Others come to Nepal to face reality. To see the world, experience the hardship and the poverty that keeps people trapped in the home. Whilst fields grow as prisons for the rural community. Working the land the farmer must struggle onward trapped by the influx of internal problems forced on them by the government and the Maoists. And is it that what we hate in others what we in fact we hate in ourselves, what we might be?

5
Stairway To The Gods

Alarm beeps, all too early, a taxi ride and another airport. The plane is a rust bucket. Will it make Lukla? From the flight I understand the frail nature of life. And the 1st city in the sky Lukla, minds blowing like the instant of 1st love butterflies and the deep smile... never to stop. The schoolboy both likes and dislikes the 1st day at school. New experiences await and the apron strings must be cut. Leaving is the hardest thing to do...

It was a bleary kind of morning; everyone was going around doing what ever it is they do to earn a crust. Back home the 9 to 5 office grind would have started and the commuters would be busy going to work. In Nepal the market vendors display objects for the weak willed and loose wallet tourist. Touts sell tours by the dozen to those that need to be shown what to appreciate rather than view with their own eyes what is of worth.

"Sir, yes sir," the mild mannered tout approaches as we load the taxi with our kayaks ready for the drive to the airport.

"You go rafting? I give you good price I know good guide, best company." I'm too busy putting the boats on the roof to notice a second man with a gap tooth smile approach.

"Tiger balm, you want tiger balm," the youth keep tapping me on the shoulder insistently to grab my attention, I just wish I'd noticed him before! Then with the art of a chat up line he lowers his voice, whispering so I have no choice but to lean into him.

"Hashish, you smokie? Good quality hashish, you want?" His persistent smothering is now getting my back up, what with the rafting tout and this small budget drug dealer working as a two some. But our minds are on something different. Without a glance I turn to talk to the small guy with the gap tooth. In a quizzical manner I explain that I don't understand him, that he must speak up a little.

"Yes Mr, you want hash? Best in Thamel," he continues. It is now a game for me, one I enjoy playing around the tourist haunts in this district of Kathmandu.

"I'm sorry I don't understand, what is Hash?" I ask in a sarcastic manner, which is missed in translation. Perhaps it's missed because even though I come to Nepal yearly I still speak in a fast Yorkshire accent. Even my long term Nepalese friends struggle to understand. It makes me smile from the inside out when they think my use of language is standard,

"Eh up lads", the oriental smiles would emulate.

"Smoke sir, natural high, take you higher," he continues. "Get high before you die," his smile widens, as he uses his best line his top spec sales banter.

"Oh get high," I spread my arms line a plane. "Like in the sky," I reply to him.

"Yes sir, high like a plane," It's still a game for me.

"You want me to get high, well that's ok my friend, I'm just off to the airport." This leaves him confused, and then I think he's got it.

"No Mr, you misunderstand, Hashish, Dope, Mar-r-r-u-a-n-a," he tries to spell it for me. The game is almost up, he might know that his time has been wasted. The best thing to do is to shout the obvious at the top of your voice hoping that the police might give him a clip around the ear. That should stop him pestering me again.

"SO YOUR SELLING HASH, POT, WACKY BACKY," I commence my verbal entourage, but he doesn't want the trouble and hot steps it into the crowed of rickshaw wallahs and taxi cabs. His friend has long since disappeared. So it's with a smile that I tie the last knot in the rope that secures the boats to the roof of the taxi.

Feeling sick in the belly, I climb into the back of the Taxi, anxious panic surrounded by the knowledge that adventures are a new start. It develops and manifests in my every thought. So many people's dreams have been pinpointed to this river. Many have left it alone not wanting to tame its rapids so why should I want to do it? As a group of paddlers with little else in common, except the dream, are we prepared? Strangely with all these emotions running high for the 1st time in a few months I'm happy, truly, with how I am and what I do, how I survive what is thrown at me. The entire avoided trauma makes one stronger avoiding false idols and demons. As the engine slowly pulled us alone the road I felt like that was a true exploration, a true expedition, not a Lads holiday in Asia as it seemed to outsiders. Perhaps its just that this mode of travel, the lonesome hours in transit and the fact that on such a river death is only one small step away from injury whilst failure is only a fraction away from success.

Kathmandu domestic terminal, a square concrete compound, no thrills, no luxury. The smell of ammonia wafts in the air. Stout guards in mix matched uniforms, with loose buttons and jackets either too large rolled at the sleeves or too small to be fastened at the waist, watch the x-ray machine click and flash as the baggage is passed through. It is a common scene where ropes and rucksacks are shunted around the terminal with the hint of disgust. No interest is shown for whoever owns such items. Our cargo is different. Our three plastic kayaks and associated kit are an awkward prospect for anyone to manoeuvre through the narrow x-ray machine and even more cumbersome to put on the scales. Even though we have chartered a Yeti Airline plane we still have to weigh the equipment. That is the bitter irony about Nepal. Bureaucracy is followed to the letter, only 'back handers', bribes, speed the process up and even then that doesn't help greatly.

The cold tiled floor offers little relief from the humid warmth enclosed within the compound. Loose wires hang from the ceiling, where once was a fan. The purpose of which was just to move the stifling air around rather than for any sort of cooling. It's only a fraction more relaxing sitting on the floor, slightly more appealing for posture than the solid plastic chairs that resonate with the retro feeling of the 1970s.

Over five hours we waited on this floor and in this crowded airport, plenty of time to think. The longer the plane is delayed on its return flight from Lukla the longer the wait. We just needed a clear weather window to take off. Over paid middle management types wait inline for the scenic mountain flights. Its not that I have a deep rooted hatred for these sort of 'holiday makers' its just that they seem out of place, flashing wallets around and handing out money left right and centre to all those that ask. It knocks out the economy of the country and produces a principal that is at some point expected of foreign visitors to Nepal.

On previous trips in Nepal it's been unfortunate that I had to share long distance bus rides with these sort of people. Through the clouds of diesel fumes those with matching travel luggage complain about the buses not running on time, or the lack of space or some other intricacies that stop the progression of movement; of travel in the developing world. What do they expect? The delays, mayhem, discomfort and irate passengers, it's all part of it, surely? As they sit in five star luxuries, in a multi-national chain hotel, the Hilton or Radisson, drinking cocktails before taking a dip in the resort pool they will claim

"Isn't Nepal such a cultured place, me and the good lady wife have really got in touch with the local people, we've feel part of it." But I wonder why? How can they feel part of it? Have they seen children too ill to be rescued with modern medication just wait to die? Have they witnessed the development of refugee camps host to thousands of Tibetans running from persecution in the land they still call home? Although I suppose that at least they have touched the surface, seen the world outside the town they were born in.

Whilst remembering something I once saw on television, lodged in the back of my mind I recall how the travel agent Thomas Cook was the first company to run trips in Nepal. I suppose this is full circle, do we learn from the past? Are we destined to make the same choices and mistakes in the future? Time will tell. Guide books map out the world explaining the best hotels and cafes. What to do and what to see is s-p-e-l-t out slowly for those who think they yearn for the adventure spirit. What is left to explore for 'yourself' someone has beaten you to it. What is left when the world on the page dictates your dreams?

Just as it looks as if our flight is about to be postponed and we will have to trail back into the centre of Kathmandu the proverbial tail between the legs, with all our expedition supplies, like so many climbing parties before, it happens. Slowly inch by inch officials gather towards the departure desk. In the corner feedback squeals from the speakers and the microphone is turned on.

"WILL THE PRIVATE FLIGHT TO LUKLA GET READY TO BOARD", well I think that was shouted in to the microphone by the uniformed official but since the entire departure hall rushed to the door and the Hendrixesque feedback continued it was hard to fathom. One by one the climbers, sight seeing tourists and those who wanted to trek in the foothills of Everest were rejected in order to await the flight they had booked.

Lukla is host to possibly the most dangerous landing and take off airstrip in the world. Having said that the flight itself isn't that safe either. Our plane, Yeti Airlines commercial flight, had been hired just for your sole use. The seats of his small aircraft hold only about 17 passengers but in order to make sure we could get the kayaks in 10 seats were taken away. As we sat in the back of the plane our kayaks took up the most part of space, that and bags of local supplies.

In order that we could get a good deal on the charter of the plane we had managed to sell the excess load space. This was economical and meant that the cargo now contained not only our supplies but also bags of rice, clothing, kerosene and food stuffs. Outside two technicians tinkered with screwdrivers on the near side of the plane. Hammers clattered in unison, we would be airborne attached to life by the turn of the screw.

The airstrip at Lukla cut deep into the mountainside as the lush green of the wooded gorge immerses the little white airline carrier. The intricate angle of entry requires that the nose of the plane stay up to avoid the lip of the tarmac. Stopping suddenly the entrance to the runway tarmac gives way to a deep void and the thin air of the Dudh Kosi gorge below. Looking down as we fly into land I notice the wreckage of a dozen or so planes that weren't lucky on the landing or take off. The twisted metal remains blot the landscape. Cast about in the air like flotsam caught in spindrift I notice Martyn reach for the sick bag. Dave is too intent on filming to laugh but I smile to myself, as too does Shiva. Shiva goes one better, he put his fingers down his throat and makes gagging noises.

"Hey Martyn, you enjoying the flight?" he asks and tries to wait for a response but he bursts into a fits of childish giggles all too soon.

Dave had known Shiva for years but he was a new inductee to Martyn and me. With a sense of humour like that he was sure gonna fit in. Dave had employed Shiva for logistic help. Shiva would hire the porters and sort out the lodges that we were to stay in. We also knew that Shiva was from the area we were kayaking in, so he had an ideal knowledge of the landscape. The game trail used by the yaks and locals would be our pathways; unmapped and not used by tourists they were Shiva's childhood playgrounds.

Joining us on the trip also meant that he could go and see his grandparents and cousin whom he had not seen for many years. Since he 'escaped' to Kathmandu to make his fortune as a trek guide, a job of social importance and high esteem. His family worked the land in a village at the lower end of the Dudh Kosi's infamous deep gorge where waterfalls crash in a succession of 40 feet cascades onto the rocks below. Mukla was only a collection of small hand build homesteads, with out road signs or house numbers. The actual spelling was uncertain, its name or at least the pronunciation was all we had to work on. Words and names get lost in translation I guess.

After seeing us on our way Shiva would fly back to Kathmandu with the supplies that we wouldn't need. On the lower river we would not need our thick down jackets or our waterproof dry trousers. I was willing to get wet for the last few days if water penetrated my boat via the spray deck, the piece of neoprene wetsuit fabric that was stretched over the cockpit seating area so we would be fully enclosed. Our spare thermals and miscellaneous items could also be flown back for us to collect from the office when we finished the trip. Shiva would take one of the porters with him to carry the stuff and I suppose to keep him company.

As a mountain and trek guide he was respected in Nepal but he carried an air of boyish character. When asked why as a Buddhist he was named after a Hindu god he replied between fits of giggles.

"Shiva is a playboy, he plays around." I guess this Shiva enjoyed playing to this social stereotype. A deity that is based on fornication and getting lucky on a Saturday night! Shiva would drink and chat up innocent backpackers at the drop of a hat.

I'd not noticed when we first met but Shiva was wearing Levi jeans and sports trainers. He carried a plastic bag and a very small rucksack. He seemed ill equipped for the high altitude walking. Having said that I was intent in walking in my Teva sports sandals so I suppose he had one up on me.

At the far end of the 100 metres or so that make up the

landing area Lukla the village in the sky starts. No roads just feet and yaks and that's it. I guess the supplies that we managed to put on our plane were a luxury. Porters are the human supply chain up in these hills, just as 40 ft lorries are on our motorways. They bring everything from the runway at Lukla or even further down near the Kathmandu valley by foot. Everything that you want is brought on the backs of men and women. Beds, Televisions, Cola, Beer, Sleeping bags, Jackets; everything is carried.

22 Oct 04
Porters are sorted and we are off up the hill from 2800m elevation, up and down the path goes. And we see the river for some time today. We are not normal trekking groups. We are not like other boating groups.

Placing one foot in front of the other we set off for the long walk. Minute after minute I feel the blood seep out of the cracks in my left foot. It's my own fault. No one else was to blame. It's a decision I made back in the UK, months ago. In order to make this trip as light as possible I had decided to walk in a pair of sports sandals with socks and shorts. Quite a sight as others on the trekking route we decked out in high support walking books poles and large rucksacks all except the porters.

The steep terrain makes the going difficult for the porters who are steady and slow, but only after a few hours we make it to the expanse of a remote hill village, the much talked about Namche Bazaar.

6
Tradition

Dust on the tracks and sweat falls into the eyes. Daily grind uphill, always pushing uphill. For once and for all human logistic trains' choo-choo, panting no letting up. Breathing in-out getting to the destination.

That's what it takes for the breathless wonder on the approach to the mystic stupas of Namche Bazaar and the places of pilgrimage, Tengboche and deeper into the Khumbu region. Alas even these high places away from roads cannot escape the trappings of the tourist trade. That's why many venture on these paths but with all the influences of the West even the sacred Sherpa community, the word translated from Tibet as the people from the East have become a generic term for people of this region. All along they are failing to hold back the advancement of modern technology.

A legend ingrained into the Buddhist tradition tells that Sagamartha, or as we call it Everest, is host to the goddess bearing food whilst a mongooses stands aside spitting diamonds and gems. In this myth of prosperity does it echo true today?

In Namche Bazaar just like Kathmandu you can get just about anything. From email access to mobile phone calls via satellite and for some that's a great thing. It's brought material wealth to the region all due to the tourist trade. Those that manage to summit on Everest and the like can now tell loved ones back home of achievements but at what cost? Its not just that female Sherpanis can listen to mini disk players whilst they do laundry in the age old manner, by the streams. Neither is it simply that the pubescent sons of these women can view the same naked images of women that American youths ogle over on Internet sites. Indeed whilst supplying email correspondence up in Namche I got chatting to the 'cypercafe' tycoon. It seems that this 'hyper-real web based centre' offered a social solution for many. This café was the place that young Nepali youths could meet, flirt and court the opposite sex. It was not in the traditional manner. Such a meeting place was far from the arrangement of marriage by parents, not a close one-on-one interaction. It is a suspended space meeting place.

Local 'singles' could look on the web for dates, picture based and with glimpses of character descriptions. 'Young female 18 seeks educated male for relationship and to be husband. Dreams of children and pleasing my family. Based in Kathmandu.' It cuts out the middleman. Social passports are available to men wanting to find a wife and new life in the city where they hope to find a future. 'Rural educated, Khunde school, 1st born son, seeks romantics life in Kathmandu.' The Hindu state still very much monogamous, with the goal of many, marriage the golden ticket in the 'Willy Wonka' tradition is 'advertised' as a prize to be relished.

Ironically it seems only a small step away from the sex that is for sale in Kathmandu to the money tourists. This resonates, reiterates the development of western influences. What is the fundamental difference between the Father asking a dowry for his daughter or the young bride putting her graces on show and the pimp selling access to the flesh of the oppressed working girl? One is justified because its part of tradition. The arrangement of a spiritual love is not spontaneous. It's a match of caste, or interests, of education and family values. Love the heart felt pounding can come later. For me at least that seems the worse of the too evils. How can a parent make a child a commodity? And it is true that neither have a choice, its just an indebted ingrained crevasse of the ideology at play one that the culture needs to claw out of.

The cost to these hill villages could be deeper, much deeper than the hyped encroachment of global westernisation where the meek are over thrown by the dominant world culture, traditions are no longer cared for. Future generations will pass without a care for the beliefs of the Dalai Lama and all that follow as his kin. But hang on, I've gone off at a tangent and into the role of a 'Free Tibet' activist, not that it's not a just cause, but it's one that requires more time than I can give, at this time.

As I walk through the valley in the shadow of death...

In the thin air the ghosts of failed expeditions hang. Talking to trek guides we hear of stories of those that have lost their lives already this year. Even with death in the air more and more people attempt the peaks. Everest alone has seen over 1600 expedition attempts since the middle of the seventies. Just fewer than 90 climbers have summated on a single day. With all these facts its seems blasé but the catastrophic unthinkable deaths still occur. In 1996 paying tourists, dispensing large amounts of money joined companies to be guided to the top. They perished as with ill experience for Himalayan climbing they succumbed to the vicious nature and apocalyptic weather. Other people site the mismanagement of the group but that is perhaps unfair. Above 28000 feet in the death zone its is surely a selfish pursuit, 2000 feet lower in elevation and the body is starting its final breakdown for death. The human system simply cannot cope.

Even so Everest draws those yearly. Climbers, kayakers, stories around the campfire also talk of some misguided French man swimming sections of the Dudh Kosi river intentionally or not since I can't remember him making it, perhaps he did. Then skiers are challenged by the off piste activities. The new millennium, 2000, October 7 Slovenian Davo Karnicar became the first person to ski uninterrupted from the top to base camp.

Even whilst we were attempting our aquatic descent word

was out about a lone female American who was attempting such a task. She was causing quite a stir with her entourage, journalists and supporters.

The beauty of the surroundings, the houses and shops cut deep into the hillside. The yaks amble alongside the paths that lead to the medical station and the rescue association buildings. Dressed in rags, faces twisted with the agony of cultural assassination, men and women wonder spinning hand held prayer wheels pushing forward with a spiritual meaning. Their eyes glazed and still smiling like the new dawn, a crisp clear dawn as viewed from high on a mountainside.

The majestic peaks, the raw power of nature and the wonders of the world are dealt before my eyes. Too much emotion to write about, it's that words cannot express the fleeting glimpses of what it's like. The closest I can get is to say that the soul is fresh as the Buddha Eyes gaze from the stupa on the marketplace where nomads sell blankets and coats, hand made and goods from India and China. Every Saturday the muddy field, scattered with the odd tuft of vegetation a weed or an alpine flower its hard to tell, is turned into an oriental film set. A 'Lost Horizon' Shangri la at 3446 metres, just over 11000 feet. Even that's not enough, it's more than words can say. Yet it is the very absence of words that make what is felt the truth, unbounded by discourse.

After finding lodgings in a log-clad hotel at the gateway to the market place we are summonsed to discuss our kayaking mission with the Park Officials and the Army. We are made to feel uneasy as the authorities probe and question us. To make dealing with the officials easier Dave does all the direct talking. Shiva acts translator. Although this I think hampers things a little. As Dave tries to resolve things with the authorities, Martyn and myself are left in limbo, gazing into the flames of the yak dung fire drinking tea, vast amounts of tea, and counting the cracks in the wooden floor. More cracks in the infrastructure as our firm plans fall by the wayside at the whim of the bureaucratic uniformed state representatives.

All day Dave was sporadic in his visits to the lodge. Each time he returned from the meetings, he looked more nervous and even tenser than before he went. Each visit resulted in Dave becoming more and more stressed. Late in the afternoon Dave returned to the lodge alone, Shiva had vanished on another agenda. Sitting down next to the fire Dave pulled out a packet of locally made fags, placing one between his lips he lit it and inhaled.

"Well were fucked lads," his dry calm tone told no signs of what was to come

"We needed a permit, we sure screwed this up."

"But all that time in the Drift Nepal Office and all the years we've spent in Nepal, you'd have thought we have heard about the permit," I said as I could feel the disappointment run through my bones.

"Yeah, well I though we'd be OK, we ain't climbing the mountain so a trekking permit seems of no concern."

"So that is the end of that…I could fucking spark you out Dave."

We sat in silence as Martyn poured more tea. Looking across at Dave I realised that I was out of order.

"Sorry…"

"Eyee…I'm doing all I can, Shiva thinks its his fault, he thinks he should have known, I'm just as pissed off as you."

"Dave I know, I'm out of order. If anything you are working like I would never believe, lets just drink this tea and see what happens ,at least we're in Namche."

"Sounds great to me, twat, you had me worried for a while. I thought we'd all fucked it then."

As we drank the tea I could still feel tension in the air. It was to be expected. After all how does a group of blokes live in each other's pockets in such closes quarters for days at a time without tensions build? No one teaches you how to cope with the dynamics of a group on an expedition, it's not an exact science especially when the expedition was like ours. We had no leader, no logistic manager, no sponsor to dictate. We were a collective on the same quest, each giving in some special way. Each of us was coping with the whole process, differently and for different reasons.

In my own way I deal with it by thinking of the past. Of near misses, of family, of friends that I no longer contact and should, of life choices that have made me whom I am today. Martyn, I know, was thinking of the future of settling down with this girlfriend and leading a normal life away from the river living lifestyle that we had all tried to avoid, but which draws us in daily. Whilst Dave was busy coping and dealing with the possibilities of working in the family business of living in a house after about 10 years of living out of a rucksack on his 'gap year'. Perhaps that scared him more than the river or the expedition.

As we all became lost in our thoughts the silence became uncomfortable, one of those pauses in conversation that goes on too long where no one dare say a word for fear of up setting the apple cart.

"Dave, you know they say we need this permit thing?"

"Yes Daz we need the permit, can't do jack shit without it."

Martyn looked up from his tea.

"Can we get one, I mean they must be available, can we get in touch with the boys in Kathmandu, with Gerry and Samir?"

Gerry knew how to pull strings. Samir is a well-heeled Nepali who owns Drift rafting operation. If anyone would be able to help these boys could. Gerry was just one of those people who you knew, who would do his best for the cause. Samir was a good friend to all of us. Back in 2002 he had helped me out financially when the shit hit the fan getting me Craig and Robin on a plane out of Nepal into India as the Maoist terrorist, a liberation army, descended on the capital.

He would do anything for anyone. They are the last hope. Our only hope it seemed.

Standing up Dave put on his down jacket finished his tea and walked out of the door.

"Don't worry I'll find Shiva, we'll sort it." Dave gave me that knowing look. The sort that only friends understand, the sort that says, 'Thanks' and 'sorry' and 'I understand' and 'yea its cool' and all that other stuff all the emotions that stop blokes from crying and hugging and seeing act uncool.

Letting the air settle in the room I looked at Martyn who gave a look to say I need space.

"I'm off for a lay down," as he picked up his tea and holding his diary in his right hand he walked down the stairs to where the bedrooms were.

Looking around I was alone. I felt empty, wanted someone to be close to. A lover, a parent, a child, but none were forth coming. In desperation, knowing that if I stayed in the lodge I would just well in self-pity, I put on my hat. Pulling the edges tightly down over the tips of my ears then putting on my down jacket I walked out of the same door that Dave had walked from 10 minutes earlier. After all the hours I'd spent waiting for news the streets seemed to offer no solace or no passion. They could have been any streets in the world. The sort of streets that you walk when, after a heated argument you leave your lover. The sort of streets that lead to no place special. The sort of streets that have seen thousands of feet shuffle along.

7
Seeing With The Blind

Higher and higher the chalk measurements plot out the growth of the schoolboy. His satchel empties and is tossed away. To gain height away from his peers he stands on a book, growing, higher, taller closer to the grown-up teachers.

Mountains are fountains, not only of rivers (...) but of men.(...), going to the mountains is going home. **John Muir.**

The streets of Namche were strangely quiet, nothing much seemed to be happening as I walked passed the market place. It was scattered with litter from the previous day's market. Trickles of water found a way to flow down the mud and stone pathways. Hopping from stone to stone I headed towards the stupa and the peace of mind that I might find underneath Buddha's eyes. I noticed Dave shaking hands with a Sherpa. Bowing then placing his palms together he utters the words 'Namaskar'. Shiva was behind standing in the shadows cast by the half open doorway. I supposed that this was yet another 'official meeting' and unseen by either of them I sloped off.

Sitting on the wall near the stupa, I gazed both into the foreground and mid distance. Below, deep in the gorge was the Nang Po/Bhote Kosi river, one of the rivers we were set to attempt. In the valley behind me the icey water of the Imja Khola took water from Everest at the Khumbu glacier and when these two rivers met just below the stupa on the steep incline that leads to Monza or Monjo the spelling and pronunciation changed all the time. The joint force of the two rivers flows towards Sun Kosi and India, becoming the Dudh Kosi. It has spent millions of years cutting a deep gorge, antecedent drainage? Or an ice age?

The eyes of the Buddha, with blue, yellow and red were

painted high on the white body of the stupa, looked in all the cardinal directions, looking and watching over the nation, over the people with wisdom and compassion. Below pilgrims and devout Buddists walk clockwise around the base. Spinning the prayer wheels attached to the loose dry stone. As the prayers echo to the soul of the heavens multi-coloured prayer flags, bleached by the aeons of time, blow in the breeze and fading light.

Followers of the ancient Bon Po religion join the Buddhist as some of the liberal Hindus join in the spinning of wheels.

"Om Ma Ni Pad Me Hum," the chorus reverberates across the Khumbu region. The district of Everest wrapped rich in a blanket of belief.

Searching for comfort and a release from the pressures of the expedition I join the chorus.

"Om Ma Ni Pad Me Hum," my dulcet Yorkshire tone seems out of place. But I continue none the less. After watching the walking mantra for a few minutes the cold rock wall is of no comfort. Standing slowly I walk without due reason towards the bottom left corner and a metal prayer wheel. I inhale the clear air steadly and exhale carefully. Focus is on the body process, the meditative calm.

"Om Ma Pad Me Hum," the mantra is repeated. My right hand flicks, keeping the motion of the metal pray wheels spinning. My fingers gently glanced against the protruding inscriptions as I walk, slowly to the next wheel.

"Om Ma Pad Me Hum." Although I know my mind should be clear and in a state of meditation I have too many thoughts. I'm drawn to my godson, What future will he have? Will I be of any use to his social development? Simultaneously I'm also pulled towards thinking of the life of Fred, my grandfather. He was a joker who for his ninety plus years on the planet brought joy and mirth to many. Having said this, he sure knew about the depression and the hard times of the proletariat struggle, but he succeeded in being compassionate to his neighbours and he never let a bad apple spoil his batch. Was he of Buddha nature to me? An unknown guru. I don't know why he was the first grandparent to come to mind? Perhaps he'd been getting close to the mantra for an indefinite amount of time, I guess so. My Nana and Granddad on my fathers side oozed into my conscience. I know that they would be tracing my journey through Asia on a globe, they liked to know what their grandchildren were doing. How the world had opened up since they were children. Travel the luxury of the modern world was a privilege that their generation could not grasp. The world was out of reach, only explorers from the upper classes or military, delved into the dark continents outside Britain. Even the rise of the British Empire didn't explore other cultures, it simply moved Britain to the Orient and Indian landmasses.

"Om Ma Pad Me Hum"..

One by one the Sherpas and Sherpanis leave the stupa, having had their fill of public religions devotions for the day. Once in the privacy of the home perhaps they will light a candle for the Dalai Lama and the cause of Buddhism on the world stage. As night closes in smoke bellows from all the houses cut deep or perched on the valley walls that surround the stupa. Candlelight warms the air, lighting the houses, even though electric lights have been available for the few years since the dawn of the solar power and way back in 1983 from a hydroelectric plant. Was it in tune with ambience that they lit oil lamps or candles or did old habits die-hard?

Climbers and trekkers make the short walk from the lodges to the local bar. Snooker table, a video screen and a jukebox playing Bob Marley and his songs of freedom. All the necessaries to enable people to drink imported beer. Again the dilution of traditions crept from the so called sophisticated world. I don't suppose for one minute that the Sherpas and Sherpanis visit that nightspot. Its all for us, the holiday traffic. Many Sherpas forgo a formal education for the dream of becoming tour guides, for us.

"Om Ma Pad Me Hum." Left alone at the stupa I walk slower but I still spin the wheels and think about the significance. What does it mean? Do I understand what I do? As candle light glows out from the lodges I think I understand. Life is struggle. It is about how we overcome the barriers that matter. What arsenal do we have to cope with all that is thrown at us? My quest this time is not for the river *per se*. That's just the vehicle that draws me close to the truth, closer to what I need to understand.

If I understood the concept of the epiphany then I suppose I'd found the secret to life. It's found too quick. It is one of the noble truths. Suffering of the body, of what happens in this reality doesn't matter. Its crass, it's a basic understanding. The quest should be hard but perhaps it had to happen to me up in Namche, so that I could understand what was to come. That is to say, that the physical and mental must suffer as its not the 'self'. The 'self' is always changing. Perhaps that's why I think of the past? Is Darren the 'self' the same person that was the one who played on his bike age 7. Did the 'self' have the same understanding of the world? Isn't it more transmigration, with each minute, the body changes; subtle changes from dead cells to new thoughts, new education. Voices in my head, but who's voices ask the questions?

"Who are you?"

"What is the point?"

"Who cares about you?"

"Should any one understand?"

It's only a sample but so many more questions echo forth in the minds eye.

With one last chorus of "Om Ma Pad Me Hum" I vow to look deeper into Buddhism, to understand, and then I wander back to the lodge. It has become dark, a translucent darkness if that's not a contradiction, unpolluted by streetlights, chemicals, car fumes or factories. I just wish I'd packed my torch as with every step my socks get wet from the water, my sandals just don't offer water proofing! And I know I look a sight with thick wool socks pocking out from under the straps of my sandals. My legs are covered with stained green thermal tights whilst a pair of ripped orange shorts conceal my modesty. Pulled down to my hips my bright yellow down jacket and blue hat finishes the outfit.

Back in the Lodge Martyn and Dave are sat chatting to some climbers on a long table at the far end of the room whilst Shiva talks to the owner. They both turn in unison. Dave spoke first.

"You ok? You look fazed. We saw you at the stupa, you've been gone hours."

"You gone all religious on us then?" Martyn said with a touch of sarcasm.

"Actually I think so. It was the strangest thing full of emotion." I didn't want to explain any more. I doubted they would really understand. I suspected my friends, Martyn at least, was ingrained into the whole Western tradition of the Christian based dogma or even the binary atheistic attitude. But I'd never inquired, I suppose that it had never cropped up in conversation.

"I'm more of a Hindu," Dave said as he lifted up the right arm of his t-shirt. Tattooed in Sanskrit was the Hindi prayer "Om Shanti". The dark blue almost black ink cut deep into his pale skin. Even though the sun is harsh at altitude and we were all suffering from burnt cheeks and had to constantly wear sunglasses, the grubby t-shirt provided the inevitable suntan line.

"I pray for peace," he said as he rolled down his shirt.

Perhaps Martyn felt out of place, unable to grasp the basic understandings of the religious connotation of Nepal or Namche or the Stupa, since he didn't respond. Head down he continued to write in his diary, we are all keeping one. A way to escape privately, a way to collect thoughts, after the event.

"Me and Shiva are sorting the logistics, I've been on email and the satellite phone back to the boys in Kathmandu. They are gonna arrange an emergency meeting with the bureaucrats that run the permit office, the officials. They are gonna try and get the law changed. If not Shiva introduced me to a Sherpa guide that thinks we could do an undercover bandit run."

"I saw you with some bloke saying Namaskar, I figured he was important otherwise it would have been Namaste, right? But if we do the bandit thing then is that for both the Imja and the Nang Po?"

"Well it's an illegal attempt, it would be the Nang Po only, but lets see what the boys can sort in Kathmandu. I will check email tomorrow, they said the meeting was later and they can't reply until the server comes back online in the morning, the office will be shut now. Anyhow we were starving so have ordered food, if you shout Shiva he will put your order in."

Taking off the hat and jacket I then went to speak to Shiva, shouting seemed so out of place in these surroundings. I put in my order from the menu. For such a remote location the menu was fine but after a few meals it was a bit bland. I mean how many variation of Nepali Curry, Dhal Bhat can you eat? And then the menu also had some food from the west. Mash, Pizza, Burger etc all of dubious taste, but how would the typical British Bed and Breakfast owner cope with cooking Nepali cuisine?

As I returned to the table I could feel my eyes begin to close. The emotions of the day were taking their toll. My head nodded, my chin touched my chest and rubbed against the sunglasses that were still dangling from the cord around my neck. In order that the glasses didn't get in the way of my hap hazard eating habits (being prone to spill anything and everything down my top at any given time), I swung the glasses so they rested on the back of my neck and the cord dangled down my chest. I was whacked and if it weren't for the fact that I'd just order potato and vegetable stew, what more could I expect, I would have gone to bed...

8
Tea Drinking, Better Thinking

All the historical words for leaders of the West, what comfort does the written script tell, 'we have nothing to fear but fear its self'. But the East, what is left for the East. None violent action is the route of the proclaimed mystic orients as the binary rolls along the highways, by the way, entrenched with the heavy caterpillar tracks of military union.

Still morning air crisp and clear. Namche was the home of lazy starts; all we could do was wait. Sitting at our favourite table near the fire we waited for our pancake breakfast and the 5 litres of hot milky tea that had become something we always ordered. What else did we have to do? Shiva still decked out in his jeans and trainers was flapping about in the kitchen, quite what all the fuss was about amused me. The lodge keeper and his wife kept pointing at us, then again at Shiva. Without reason it seemed Shiva had a new occupation, a waiter? He brought out our food and as we tucked in with relish he stared impatiently. I suspect that he'd been out into the market of the streets this morning, His mirrored sunglasses, bought in Kathmandu and a cheap fake copy, balanced on his head. Looking like a second set of eyes, fly like. All was not well.

"What is it Shiva, *kasto chha,*" Dave asked breaking into Nepali when he felt that the person he was speaking to demanded respect or would respond to a local dialect.

"*Tikk chha, OK,* Mr Crazy Dave, Daas, Marteeeen, things are not good," his voice was agitated. Something was on his mind. He was struggling to find the worlds in English to express what was happening.

"When you all went for a walk yesterday, you know when you went for water you were only gone for a few minutes. Well the army came to the lodge they began questioning the owners asking if you were still here and what was happening?"

"We are waiting for Dave to collect the email," I said between each mouthfull of stodgy flour pancake.

"They don't want you in Namche, every one knows...you are not how you say...unknown...invisible...They are watching you. It's the Kayaks, they stand out. It's the responsibility, er they er emmm..."

"Don't like, like don't want it in their park, is that it Shiva..." I asked.

"Sorry, it so is," his brown eyes dropped, he looked sad.

"Shiva its OK, don't panic it will all come clean in the wash. How do you say it? *Ke gar nee? Bandi Bayou?* - What to do? It's all habit." Dave was putting on a brave face but we all knew, inside things were bad, worse than bad. All the planning, all the efforts to come to Nepal and to come to the river of our dreams were fading fast. The river that had drawn us to the Kingdom of Nepal in the first place might be out of reach.

Our situation was tense and we had only just woken up, we sure wondered what the rest of the day is going to bring. Our porters sat motionless in the corner of the room. All three poorly dressed. They wore cheap flip-flops on their feet. Calluses and dry skin, broken toe nails and scars showed the ravages of the work these feet had done. Working from the bottom up they all wore loose fitting trousers. Either cotton roughly stitched with patches or some manmade fabric. On their top halves one wore an old jacket from a western suit, the pockets were loose and the stains and stench from the cloth should have resigned it to the sealed containers used for nuclear waste disposal. The other two were just as badly decked out in threadbare tank tops and sport leisure jackets from the 1970s. A clothes donation perhaps, from an aid organisation.

Shiva had personally hand chosen the porters since they were from the village where we were due to rejoin the river at the end of the portage we expected. Using the information that Gerry had given, we knew we would have to walk around a deep sheer sided gorge. The porters would be of much needed assistance here. Once back on the river they could then go back to the family they no doubt missed, since they spend every available day working away for so long. Having said this, it reminded one of the porters we had employed on the Arun expedition a few years earlier. The chief porter, the Sidar, upon leaving the road head and the inevitable week long walk, said good bye to his wife and children no doubt saying that he would be home in about 10 days (walking without a load was often quicker). 4 Days into the walk we were forced to stop at mid morning as he visited a tea house, a mud and thatch rural lodge that offered simple food and hot milk tea. Whilst showing great affection to the *didi*, lady of the tea house, he played with the children before leaving again.

Since public affection is frowned upon in Nepal, we could only assume that it was another wife or mistress and the urchin-faced offspring were his. In some old book about the High Himalayas I remember reading that Sherpa men and the porters from near the Khumbu area take more than one wife or a concubine. We didn't ask, he didn't tell, so I suppose it was not out business.

Our porters for the Dudh Kosi expedition had been given an advance in wages. I supposed that whist we were laid up in Namche, doing what looked like nothing special they were concerned about the future employment prospects. Did we need them to carry down and back on a plane at Lukla? Were we going to pay them or would we try to cut another deal and cease their employment.

"Look guys, let me finish this fag, take a shit, then I will email, can you sort the bill Daz?"

"Sure Dave, we'll wait for you...just mind that squat and drop, you don't want shit on your shoes"

"Narr, it saves hitting the fan." Then he was off.

Perhaps it was the altitude but I found this funny and cracked a small smile in the corner of my mouth. In these times of desperation I suppose anything can be funny. Even though the lodge had a western style sit down toilet me and Dave preferred the squat method, since we had no paper the age-old douche method was the best option.

Sipping every cup of tea slowly we waited for news from Dave. It was like the father waiting for his wife to give birth. I paced up and down the corridor of the lodge. Martyn kept trying to relax and lay down on the benches. As for Shiva, he was sat on the steps of the Internet café smoking Dave's fags. Before he lost the glow from the tobacco he would re-light a new one. I knew that Dave would do the same if he could. That is if he'd not left his fags on the table for Shiva to 'borrow'.

As the minutes ticked by, tick-tock-tick-tock elaborating the sound track of the climbers who were content on venturing up the mountains surrounding Everest. Hourly more people booked into the lodge, our home. Dressed in top spec Gore-Tex jackets and walking poles they seemed to have all the gear but were they just one of those parties that has all the gear and no idea? Adventure tourists or did they know what they were doing? Trying to work their way up the network of influential climbers? I figured that they fell into the latter camp since they had no guide or porters. They were a self-supporting expedition. I just wished them success. After looking Martyn and myself up and down they grouped together at one of the smaller tables near the windows looking out over the market place and dusty streets. Getting out maps and guide books they began to discuss various routes and the time schedule, at least that's what I think they were discussing as I half listened to their German tones. What did they think of us? Did we look as rough as we surely felt?

It had been a good while, a week or so, since I'd taken a

proper shower. The same was true for Martyn. I'd had the same clothes on since I arrived in Kathmandu. In fact I'd had the same clothes on since I'd changed in the service station in London, just off the M25, on my way to collect Martyn and Kelly his girlfriend on the drive to the airport.

My hair felt dirty and although short I could feel it matting. Over time with nothing to do I ran my fingers through it. Such actions produced an avalanche of dust and dirt that fell into my eyes. If I was lucky the perspiration on my forehead would catch it and the marinade could be wiped onto my already filthy T-shirt or onto my sleeping bag, depending whether it was day or night.

Before lethargy overtook me I stood up glancing out of the window, the world was going on as normal. I ordered yet another flask of tea. Asking for extra cups in case the porters wanted to join me in sipping this concoction. I started to pour, what else to do? Although the British were famous for tea drinking this was ridiculous; in the last few hours we'd managed to ingest about 6 litres all of which came from the florally decorated metal flasks with a cork top loosely resting on top.

Whilst pouring a second cup from the flask Dave returned; he looked down trodden and cast out to dry. Fumbling in his pocket I assumed he was searching for his fix of nicotine. I continued to pour the cup and with arms outstretched I offered it to Dave.

"They've done what they can, but the law stands, Samir said that the meeting was so tense and....well they ...well...backs against the wall. Gerry is going to email later but at the moment we have nowt to do...well.. change plans again, its... like what to do." Bringing the tea to his lips, cupping the brew with both hands he sipped at his tea.

"Shiva you got my fags, bastard." As we watched Shiva cast the soft pack of indiscreet Nepali cigarettes across the table. Shaking one out Dave looked at Shiva; had he insulted him with the words? Swearing was common between us, it's a lads tours type thing. No kids around and who were we going to offend? We all understood the spirit it was intended, it was part of our language, part of what we did. Shiva I guess just thought it was normal. Cheekily he reached for the last remaining cup. Lifting the flask he shook it to see if any liquid was left. Before taking off the cork top and pouring the remnants into his cup.

"Lets just finish this brew and go for a walk," Dave said as he lit the cig between his lips.

"Eyeee, a bit of air, lets check out the river." My Yorkshire tones echoed off the wood lodge.

Looking like the deformed half brothers of the legendary three musketeers we stood as a group dictated to by circumstance. Walking, our aching aphasia bodies lurched into the dusty narrow alley that was classed as a street. In the fresh air, away from the claustrophobic atmosphere of the lodge, we all wore shorts and thermal tops over which we had our T-shirts. Martyn was the smartest of all with his almost clean blue shirt. With chest pockets still creased from a miss-placed iron, I suspected. The shirt complimented the light blue thermal won next to the skin and red shorts. He was a catwalk traveller opposed to the nomadic, tramp like appearance that myself and Dave showed. We each wore ageing wool hats with loose threads that escaped the knitted pattern, like the stray hair of primary school girls as they struggle with retaining the locks behind 'Alice bands' and cheap elastic tie backs. Our thermals and shorts were stained from years of world travel and over use. We all wore sunglasses and due to the exposure to the sun were developing white rings around our eyes. Each of us had a goatee beard. Mine never trimmed or tamed, even in the UK, even for work was only marginally better than Dave's. Alas Martyn's facial hair had obviously seen its share of razors and styling.

Avoiding the yak excrement scattered on the streets, the narrow pathway was a gauntlet that needed to be run. Between the random splatterings were piles of the stuff drying in the sun ready for the fire. Up in this dry and arid landscape timber was a luxury that was used for building first and warmth later. The dried faeces offered just as much heat and aroma all of its own.

Chatting in the colourful doorways were residents of Namche. Idle in stature, passing the time, gossiping. The asexual faces smiled, a gap-toothed smile, whilst beads rotated through the fingers of the right hand. Women dressed quite traditionally adorned with shell necklaces, remnants from Tibet when it was at sea level can you believe it. These gems from the maritime environment hung around wrinkled necks brushing against the stripped apron strings. All was traditional with the addition of running shoes.

Yellow, Orange, Purple, Red and Blue paint decorated the window sashes and roof tiles. Whilst kaleidoscope illusions of the rainbow flutter with the minimal breeze, gaily strung as the reverence of the prayer flags high in the foreground set against the pale blue sky.

The path-traversed north towards Everest first veering right then left uphill of the market place. Arching past the Himalayan Rescue Association building and medical station. As we walk, gasping for air in the altitude the onset of altitude sickness could be felt as the brain swells causing nausea and simple headaches for some. The stupa stares inquisitively with its painted eyes behind us, able to see all. My feet, still bloody with every step, shuffle more than walk. Its too much effort. Why did I want to leave the comfort of the lodge and the selection of books, even the Bible was offering me something to read, something to do that required no energy if not least as a reference. It was a book I had never had much time for. Fifteen minutes pass, and the walking takes us passed the intricate craftsmanship of the mani walls whilst more prayer wheels are evident, spun as we walk along side. I felt enriched, tired true, but enriched like I guess I should, having connected with the feeling at the stupa. Perhaps others just used it as a cliché photo opportunity.

Delicate stone carvings, the edifices whitewashed against the grey stone, are prayers given for the spirits as visual representations. A 'tablet' if you like, akin I suspect to the Ten Commandments of Biblical ethics. But unlike the ones with rules, that Moses self-righteously delivered to the masses from the Mount Sinai direct from God, Buddhist belief systems grant the seemingly inanimate object to the gods in the making and reading. That's the difference, the giving of blessings rather than the receiving from some other, higher being. The gods of Buddhism, however magnificent and splendid with the celestial realms more wondrous then can be conceived by the mind of the lay-man, are governed never the less by the same basic laws as of those on the mortal coil. Enlightenment, the path of understanding changes the mind set. It is not an out of body after life its here in this place available to all. The Buddhist doesn't have to wait for the call of judgement day.

Similar religious-spiritual characteristics we had encountered every mile or so whilst walking from the airstrip. It seemed so long ago. As we wandered we noticed the protocol the right and proper way to walk, for the believers or none believers, to the right or to the left. Just like at the stupa we tried our best to follow and honour the traditions since every bit would help us in our quest. Superstition or belief, fact or fiction such practices became our mascots.

Disappearing up towards the remote settlement of Khunde the little path continued its age old route. The multi-coloured flags have being raised since the dawn of time along this route, or simply since cotton dye colours were made I cynically suspect (although natural dues should not be forgotten).

The peaceful symbol of the belief system is set free in the skies. For about the last 30 years above the village the coloured cloth has been flying into the heavens in memory of Louise and Belinda Hillary, Sir Edmund Hillarys wife and daughter who tragically died in 1975 in a plane crash en route to the Khumbu. The same year I was born.

The flags and the mani walls, if nothing else, present a physical sign for the peace and compassion that I for one strive toward. It is as much to say this is both within ourselves and projected outwardly. It is the life blood of the Himalayan ranges, of the religion and the region. At no point in history has this been more apt, more to the point. Over the border, as European kayaker Salvato writes in Dave Manby's book 'Many Rivers to Run', in the still very bounded Tibet, a war is waged. It's been over 50 years since China collided into Nepal engulfing the autonomous region that is Tibet. As the Polata Palace fell to ruin and Tenzin Gyatso His Holiness the 14th Dalai Lama fled into exile to India. The cultural hegemony of Chairman Mao and his Little Red Text Book reclaimed Tibet to the Motherland.

A daily political end game, a continuation in process in which the dominant class does not merely rule a society but leads in through moral, ethical intellectual and educational powers. It's a not so subtle penetration of power.

Mao's communism whilst understandably simple on paper, understandably fair and equal to all, was never as it seemed. Mao's promises of integration to the motherland whilst still keeping dignity and tradition for the people of Tibet was never followed through. The campaigns for Free Tibet constantly highlight the warped senseless acts undertaken by Chairman Mao and his red army for the cause of peace and stability in the motherland. Mao followed the philosophy of Karl Marx to the letter.

Reaching back into the darkest corners of my academic mind I question what even I was taught at University based on Marx's essay of 1844. Quoting from 'Toward the critique of Hegels philosophy of right'. Marx put it thus. "Man is the world of man, the state, the society. This state, this society produce religion, [...] a perverted world". It sounded so simple, 'we' are alone. Mao wanted all that Buddhism offered gone, the peace loving, unarmed pacifist people could put up no resistance. His none-religious utopia was the masthead of his communist dominant ideology. Even now with the seat of the Tibetan government in hiding and monks and nuns brutally raped, beaten and killed using British and American made weapons no fight or civil war is waged. Perhaps the most horrific punishment is the much portrayed use of electric cattle prods, the ones that send a shock when attached to the skin, whilst they burn at the flesh. It has been documented that these 'weapons' are inserted, for the purposes of buggery and sodomy into anuses, vaginas, mouths and ears of the detained monk's and nun's whilst other punishments include the crushing of testicles and horrors more graphic that I don't care to think of. Such pain leaves the victims speechless and often dead or maimed. I'd read in 'Storms of Silence' by the climber Joe Simpson how nuns and monks were made to have intercourse together or with prostitutes. Such acts destroying the sanctity of Tibet. The communist drawn monstrosities were greater perhaps than the Nazi holocaust or the horror and destruction of Cambobia, not least because the world knows little about this struggle, the world cannot morn for it does not understand.

Perhaps the bitterest pill to swallow is the simple fact that these saffron robed devotees have done nothing wrong except carry photos of the Dalai Lama and follow the Buddhist doctrines and teachings. Even after all the pain and suffering the Tibetan people don't resist the onslaught that happens daily. Is that true compassion?

Even after the Chinese authorities have systematically tried to 'educate' Tibet into the teachings of the 'Little Red Book' and the motherland, many ethnic Tibetans still remain as prisoners caged within the country they were born to. Fear drives many as they try to escape becoming refugees in Nepal, Bhutan or India. The tiny dusty path upon which the mani ways and prayer flags stand is one way out of Tibet into Nepal. Crossing in the harshness of winter is the safest. Few 'security patrols' and border guards brave the sub zero climates. Alas the often poorly dressed refugees must, if they want a chance for freedom.

Back in 2002 I'd visited a refugee school in Nepal and the stories I heard amazed me. Even the simplest story of the school system shocked me. I was awash with the horror and anguish. I researched the plight so my memory finds it hard to distinguish between the people I talked to and the accounts I read after the event.

The Principal of the school, I remembered his tired face and white cotton shirt as he put a silk scarf over my shoulder, told the story. Walking so close to Tibet, as I was, in order to put this expedition to rights. Was the altitude making me hallucinate? Was the conversation as real as I remembered? Was it somehow a conversation I was remembering from a book? I sure remembered walking into the refugee camp. The heart felt kindness and the pictures of the Dalai Lama on the wall. I remember the students rushing out to buy me a coke from the roadside even though I never asked for one. They wouldn't even accept money for it. The old Tibetan women with gold rings in the nostrils, how could I forget?

"As you may know sir," the Principal, in his late thirties I guessed, bowed. "We are a loving people, we believe in reincarnation, we don't hurt anyone...its your phrase I think, you say wouldn't hurt a fly? Well we don't." His English was much better than mine was and indeed I spoke no Tibetan and little Nepali.

"How does this effect the education in China...I mean Tibet...Occupied...Oh sorry." I remember feeling embarrassed by my lack of knowledge.

"It is still Tibet for the people, in our hearts...One of my pupils was learning at school, like a good boy...all Tibetan boy good...the teacher was from China. One day she asked the pupils, for homework to kill an animal and bring it in. The child who managed to kill the biggest animal would get an A".

"Yes," I said, reliving this conversation, the clarity even if I had read the words someplace else, they could have been issued from the mouth of the teacher.

"Well the boy, was a Buddhist, he didn't want to kill anything. It was against his belief."

"I understand."

Putting his hand firmly on my shoulder, pressing his fingers into my collar bone, he continued.

"I don't think you do, with respect. The boy killed a fly. He got the lowest mark in the class and the cane." I have visions of him mimicking this action with his own hand and a broken ruler before he continued the tale.

"But worse, he knew that the fly could have been a person once. How could he have killed someone? He was forced to."

"He was forced to," those words sat in my throat. Weren't the members of the Communist Army forced to obey the orders of Mao? The compassion, perhaps I was starting to understand. How did the western capital world manage to avoid doing anything? Sure, during the rise of the British Empire and for the sake of expansion 'we' had made our share of world destruction and domination. Things were different now, surely.

9

Time And Again

The tears fall from the sky, discontentment is of the appeal. Sagamartha is not content to sit and watch the world around her fall to pieces. She doesn't want what is left of her virgin flesh groped by man for his own self worth. Thinking for number one, the plight of the man-child is born and will die alone. What happened to all for one and one for all?

Beep-beep-THE FINANCIAL CENTER OF AMERICA HAS COLLAPSED

Beep-beep-DOWN WITH THE DOLLAR-DOWN WITH THE CAPITALIST

Beep-beep-TURN ON THE NEWS.

My phone had been beeping for the last ten minutes. I'd been typing random text into my mobile phone, but I was on the wrong wavelength. I'd missed the news on the lunchtime program, too busy listening to the 'country' music of Gram Parsons. It was years ago yet still in the minds of Americans and Britons.

It all started on one day in Middle America when two jumbo jets crashed headlong into the twin trade towers. At first all the worlds media could not grasp how such an accident might occur but as the dust settled and the screams of pain ceased, people died as the reality-hit. It was no accident; it was a simple Terror attack. Could attacks of such nature ever be simple?

It was claimed that a bearded Islamic Militant, Bin Laden, was the mastermind behind the destruction. He wanted an end to American Capitalism world-wide. My mind rushed headlong through the facts, briefly trying to be coherent, trying to condense them and run a parallel to the location I was in. Walking in silence, so close to the border of Tibet, wandering in a country that was at ends with its own advancement for modernisation.

George W Bush, the president of the USA stood on the TV, his words required at a time of national disaster echoed with the vibrations of the leader of the Third Reich. Just Like Hitler speaking prior to the Second World War. Hitler had said, "My patience is now at an end" and now Bush could have voiced the words. Proclaiming that he would not stand back and watch the world succumb to terror. He vowed to combat terror in all its forms around the world. How was he to succeed without becoming a dictator himself? Why was he still selling arms to China? Why did he not come to the help of the Dalai Lama?

For months Allied forces battled in Central Asia, in the Hindu Kush looking for the elusive Bin Laden. He could not be found and the conspiracy theorists started to discuss the propaganda; did America 'fix' the attack? Did Bin Laden appear as he seemed? We all waited with baited breath; no answers came. Then without warning Bush, in charge of the Allied troops; turned to attack an old enemy. The ruthless leader of Iraq became the target. Bush and Blair told the world they were set to 'out' him for his 'use of' or 'his holding of' or 'his manufacture of' weapons of mass destruction. The reasons for going to war were uncertain. What justification did they have to dispel the world of fundamentalists, Islamic jihad?

In hindsight the CIA knew that the information and intelligence was flimsy. The greatest world super powers were up against the wall. I was one of the citizens that stood back and did nothing. The battle of fundamentalism was a double-edged sword, its their ideology, their cause what democracy. It was a battle of cowboy movie proportions, the good versus the bad. The West modern world with technology and financial security against the East with firm religious views and misunderstood doctrines.

Troops powered by Bush rolled into Iraq where culture was

destroyed and innocent people got in the firing line. Iraqi detainees were tortured just like those under the influence of China.

With the Allied forces occupying the Middle East and bringing peace to the region, Bush was adamant on occupying Iraq, taking power from Saddam Hussain and ruling as an interim government. Stripping back the country to the bare bones so that it could be rebuilt. Stripping the flesh from the bones, isn't that what Mao did both literally and figuratively? What did Mao do different, why is no one holding an advertised weekly demonstration outside the American embassy as they do for Tibet, outside the Chinese Embassy in London. Although it is true that Brian Haw has set up camp in Parliament Square in London to protest against bombing Iraq, he has been in his camp in protest again the 1st Gulf conflict in since 2001. He is on the edge of society for his bit of freedom, having lost his wife and kids due to what he believes. But are people listening to him? Do people not just think he is a vagrant?

Tibet is a well-documented case but years before, before the foot soldiers marched the crushing path. Before the holocaust was cast like the Storm troopers and SS of the Nazi era. Xinjiang fell, the far West region of China as it borders Pakistan, split only by the K2 massif. Isn't that what's so wrong with the Maosit cause, the so-called liberation army of the people of Nepal, those who rule by fear and a dissident civil war.

As bodies froze on top of Everest the kingdom of Nepal buckled under its own civil uprising. In excess of 7000 people brutally killed during clashes between the Royal Nepalese Army, civilians and the Liberation Army-Maoists since the middle of the 1990s. Although the Sherpa people offer little support for this Peoples war' a nightly curfew remains in Namche and other places around Nepal. These are concerns for us and yet another concern for the authorities at large.

Sitting on the cold rocks surrounded by mani walls we looked down to the river, the wind on my back, quiet. Dave is smoking, sucking hard through the filter tip. Martyn takes photos on a small waterproof camera whilst my camera sits in its tough waterproof box. I intend to use it later but at the moment so many things are on my mind, if I cannot focus my thoughts so how will I manage to focus the SLR cameras zoom lens.

"Look guys, the lines in the river, it's a hard class 4, impassable but over near the far bank," Dave was keen to point out the way he suspected we could run the river.

"Yeah, cut past the first boulder and then track over to the middle of the flow, its clean all the way...but we cannot see what is going on directly below"

"I know Daz, but I guess we just take the chance," Dave was still enthusiastic, still keen. But Martyn, in his silence he told how he wasn't happy. Sure we were a few hundred meters up and the rapids were huge, but the lines the easy path as some would call it was also proportionally large.

Taking out my camera I took token snaps of the river, soaking in the surrounding before I just wanted to return to the lodge. Although the day had been clear I could see clouds roll over the hills at the side of the gorge. I could feel rain in the air, smell it. I wanted to be safe in doors. Did the monsoon that stops raining in September still have a bit of liquid to dispense? Was the holy mountain unhappy as the folk-lore and myths tell? When great storms descend from her summit the goddess, Sagamartha-Everest cries.

10
Damp Dream

The green eyed yellow idol gazed down. What did it matter to the mortal moral soil that I walked. What did any of this matter to those that passed on? Three score and ten is all we have to prove our life, so they say, and the problems arise on how best to spend it? Between right words right mind and right action what held onto the soul as the body plodded on to the daily grind.

On the slow walk back from the mani walls and the odd photographic moment we had walked in silence. My thoughts alone were of this new chapter of what could be. I did not know what would happen. It was simple. Climbers and walkers mingled with the locals and through the curtain doorways of shaggy looking wooden buildings the porters and local guides drank chang and rakshi, the local 'home brew'. Shiva was among them. It's a high altitude networking possibility but with each deal he struck it would be inevitable that he would become more and more drunk. As each bottle was cast aside, each pint pot empty Bob Marley again strained through the speakers, singing songs of freedom. We walked past. Coffee became our tipple, for once we craved the security of hanging out with the tourists in the custom build 'café and bar' complex. It was a melting pot of the western world. We met a couple of guys that were intent on cycling around the world. They talked of Cambodia and shooting livestock for fun. A pilot from the USA told how the flight to Lukla, the one we had taken a few days previous, was one of the hardest in the world. He talked about training flights on a computer simulator and how he crashed every time. It was reassuring to know of others were as enthralled as we were with Nepal and the chaos theory that seemed to be living day by day.

People, familiar dialects and accents although comforting did little to stop the nervous butterfly farm in my stomach. Rain was falling from the sky, large puddles were cast in the footpaths and below the stalls of the traders. No doubt this influx of water was raising the already spate possibilities of the rivers.

Six feet high and the rain its washes north and south, no use looking for higher ground. Dropping, saturating, bringing us down with it. From the memories of wet windy holidays, ruined, to spoilt playground games as a child. Dragging its heels my mind was sinking.

The lodge that had become our advanced base camp, the expedition head quarters and our sole resting-place. It was also the place where problems were found, where tension built up in our bodies. We were living in each other's pockets. We, although individuals, were one unit. We were one homologous face sent on the task in hand. If Dave coughed I felt it, when I felt down no doubt the others did too. That's what happened when we were in the lodge, alas it is the plight of those on expeditions.

So we were again sat on the neat embroidery cushions of the lodge, apathy in the air and a feeling of loosing. We felt like underdogs with our goal slipping slowly out of reach. We had to clutch at straws if we were to find away out. A way to salvage the expedition. Between the smoke of both cigarettes and the fire, speaking softy and with stealth like the dominance and austere figure of the lonesome Sherpa kept council with us. Dressed in a smart polo style shirt and jeans he would not have been out of place in a golf club where I guess he would be propping up the bar with a slim gin and tonic at the 19th hole.

His name I didn't catch and through half whispers he talked of how he could assist this failing expedition.

"It will be ok, the river is easy not rapid, flat just bouncy," his smile although perhaps out of place was reassuring. His olive coloured hands made simple wave movements as if to indicate that the river would be just a wet bouncy castle. Some aquatic funfair ride perhaps?

"So we can go, its easy to get us to the river," Dave continued to ask.

"Sirs…porters will carry your equipment in the night…not dangerous they will hide the rafting next to the river…very simple sirs then in the morning you dress as climbers and collect the boats and go rafting, class 2 like Trisuli." It seemed a simple plan and although our new found conspirator within the Sherpa community was saying raft rather than kayak we all understood. The Trisuli was a bench mark for Nepal rivers it was one of the 1st rivers commercially rafted in the country and it draws backpackers daily on commercial trips to its bouncy waves and white foam hydraulic jumps.

"IT IS NOT LIKE THE BLOODY TRISULI, Shiva it's not easy it's hard that's why its never been done, we can see the lines from up here but at water level I just don't know…" Dave was loosing his cool but not wanting to upset the other occupants of the lodge he kept his voice down. Shouting softly if that was at all possible. More negotiation kept coming from out of the mouths of our hosts. "Shiva it's a tourist run, the Trisuli, punters pay, it's easy…"

The whispers drew a similarity with the playground rumours of yester-year. The whispers kept insisting that the river, the whole of the river, would be class 2 like the Trisuli. But how did he know? I doubt that he had ever been to the Trisuli, why should he have? I began to feel uneasy, were we being dictated to. Did our host understand what was happening?

"Daz," Martyn murmured in my ear, "we need to talk, outside." I sensed he was shaken and if nothing else nervous.

"Dave, me and Martyn are off for some air, see ya in a bit." Collecting our jackets we left the lodge and sat on the step of the closed gift shop opposite. The night air wasn't as crisp as usual, rain fell from the sky, dripping from the broken roof gutters of the buildings.

"What is it Martyn?" I asked but I had already guessed. Martyn I suspected felt uncomfortable, unable to deal with the changes in plan, unable to adapt, unable to allow the Nepali host a way to assist. He was a voice piece for the Sherpa tradition and knew that, perhaps, we would look on him to provide a background to his culture. Unlike Dave and myself, Martyn wasn't fully coerced in the oscillation of emotions, of the ever changing plans and pitfalls of expeditions. It's a common phrase that you cannot be on an expedition unless you are suffering!

"I don't like it, Shiva, I think is trying to rush us, trying to get us down the river as quick as possible...I think he just wants us out of the way. He just wants to get to his family and we are paying, listen to him he's half pissed." Looking across at Martyn, I diverted from his gaze. I feared that behind his small fashion glasses his eyes would be full of rage or worse terror. If terror was surrounding Martyn what would I do? What would happen to the expedition if he wanted to call it quits, call it a day cut his losses and go home? I could find so few words to comfort.

It was true Shiva had been slurring his words all afternoon and we had seen him drinking chang, the local brew with some other guides when we returned from looking at the rapids, echoing below.

"I know Martyn, but if we want a crack at the river then we have to listen...I know its not the best option and that the Imja would have been what we came for...."

"It's not happening, this isn't the plan, this isn't why I'm in Nepal."

"I know but we can't do what we came for...at least we are getting the Dudh and the Trib in. It's all out of our area of experience. Out of our control."

"It's not the same..." I could hear disappointment in his voice.

"Look lets see what Dave has to say, we can talk about it as a group."

Dave was still heavy in conversation with Shiva and the Sherpa when we returned. Looking at Dave, square in the eyes I flicked my head towards the bedroom we shared. I knew Dave would follow as we shuffled into the bedroom. Martyn sat on one bed, I pushed up my sleeping bag and dry bag containing a thermal top and my toothbrush so that there was space for Dave to sit down. Dave followed.

"We need to talk Dave," I said, knowing that being diplomatic was the best option. Diplomacy was never a skill that I had much call for. I called a spade a spade and was always honest. It was also true that earlier I treated to punch Dave spark-out. It was frustration. Way back at the start of the trip, in the pubs of Kathmandu, I said that if such a stressful encounter were to happen, then I didn't mean it. Such an outburst was just the onset of expedition stress. Just a way to fight against the expeditions close unit nature.

Perhaps it was my weakness, it often seemed that my internal monologue didn't function properly. I'd never seen the point in talking behind people backs or being subtle. Against my normal manners I turned blindly to the caring sharing, lefty liberal side that I reserved somewhat strangely for my work as a child care worker.

Strangely no tension was in the air. And yet my heart was beating like the wings of a humming bird in a cage.

"We've been talking," I pointed towards Martyn it was after all his concern, I was just a mouthpiece since Dave was more my friend than his. "The river ain't going to be like the Trisuli, if we get into difficulty then we are fucked and the police and army will surely clamp down on us. What about the guys that are gonna help us attend this illegal jaunt? Won't they get a good arse shafting?" It was a bad turn of phrase but one that had been used so often to describe the horrors of the Nepali penal system that it seemed apt.

"I understand," Dave replied calmly "I'm just trying to salvage a bit of hope for the trip."

"And Shiva he's pissed, I think he just wants us to get to his family" Martyn piped up, perhaps a little out of place.

"Look Martyn, I've known Shiva for years he's my mate, he'd never fuck us about. He's just doing his best. If he can say that he worked with us, as friends and clients like this then that's kudos for him and the company he works for, for 'Drift and Trek Nepal' back in Kathmandu. It's a big thing." Dave was keeping a cool head. He understood that things said on expeditions were sometimes taken out of context, in the heat of the moment. "I've already sent an email to Gerry for more ideas, to see what he suggests."

"Lets just go back up to the boys and ask them about what would happen if we attempted the illegal run? What would happen if we were caught or the porters were spotted?...it's worth asking that might be the end to reason, if nothings going to happen to us then its worth the gamble. Pay a bribe to the army should they spot us and then we are on our way...top eh?" I was optimistic having said these words that should nothing happen to us and we'd only loose a little bit of cash as a bribe then the gamble would pay off.

If you can keep your head...as all around...friends looses theirs. Mirror images and broken glasses stained with the ravages of time. Loose spent ash from the cancer sticks sit stagnant in the aftermath of the last nights party...its over. The party is well past its best. It's over...

Raising the metal cup to his lips Shiva was drinking black tea with the Sherpa helper and the porters when we returned to the communal dining area of the lodge. Our porters sat motionless with backs to the wall. Each had their hands laid softly across their knees. Eyes were cast down, no words could escape from their lips. Without saying a word they all looked nervous and with blank expressions like they were awaiting a firing squad at dawn.

The conversation between the austere Sherpa and Shiva was too fast for us to understand. The dialect is too strong, not slowed for unaccustomed ears. They spoke in fast dialogue. Never raising voices, quiet Nepali phrases became indistinguishable from the Hindi and broken English that they used. To compound the situation and the anxious nature of our predicament I feel excluded and this feeling I'm sure pervades to all of us. Even Dave who prides himself on being able to understand the native tongue and reply accordingly was at a loss. We were outcasts of our very own situation. We, it seemed, were talked about but never asked our opinion. Paranoia over took. I could feel eyes burn into my back. I could feel how foolish we had become, how we had thought we could just fly from the UK and attempt the river without cause, without duress, without really knowing, without reconnaissance. Who were we trying to kid?

Joining in the conversation would have been difficult, we could not asses the correct pause to enable us to join in naturally. Rude and abruptness, my forte, would be the only answer.

"Shiva, we need to know," my dulcet Yorkshire tones echoed around the room acoustically bouncing from the wooden walls. Politeness wasn't going to be my strong point. Although I figured Dave would have used a more peaceful tact. I had so many questions that needed to be asked and so, so many answers that needed to be honest. "What would happen if we got caught? Can we use bribes? What would happen to us? Or to you and the boys?" The barrage of questions must have come as a shock to Shiva.

Dave reiterated the points and again. Shiva was off talking in fast Nepali to the Sherpa conspirator. Minutes passed, as it seemed half the lodge stared into space just waiting in limbo. For our part would the expedition get off the group and onto the river? For the porters would they still have work? Would Shiva be able to look after his 'clients'?

"It is quite simple but nothing to worry about, ke gar nee, what to do." Shiva said as he turned to us and smiled. He seemed jovial, without cause for concern.

"I must answer the questions honestly," he spoke calmly but the smile eased from the corner of his mouth. "You would be put in prison or deported without cause. I would not be allowed to work as a trek guide, it is likely that we would all be in a fight.."

"You mean beaten?" Dave interjected.

"Yes, thats its, sorry my English is poor." Shiva seemed apologetic as he continued in his calm tone. He seemed obviously worried, but I could sense that we had to make the final decision. He would help us and support our choice, whatever may become of it.

"Maybe killed, they could do that to you, the army could and blame it on the Maoists. But it's your expedition, we can only help, we all know the consequences. We have known for days but didn't want to scare you. We all want the expedition to be a success."

"Wow Shiva, how could you keep this from us, how can we go on now." Disappointment ran through my body. But I had to keep a cool head, had to understand what was a stake. How they were all willing to put their lives on the line for some English adventurers. Martyn became even more withdrawn and sat alone in silence putting his thoughts into his diary. A book of events he was going to give to Kelly, when he couldn't tell her the whole story. Dave just flicked yet another creased and roughly made local cigarette from his packet that he tucked in his hat.

My mind kept flashing to the books I'd read about prisons and hostage situations world-wide. How Amnesty International seemed defenceless and yet I wanted to run this river so much but I wondered was it worth more than life itself? Was it worth the risk to life even before we got on the river? How did the boys our employees feel? We had a duty to them after all. Could anything be salvaged? Turning back was no option at all. We already sacrificed our chance to see the sacred the mythical monasteries of the high Khumbu tradition. We had missed the ice-capped peaks since we were not going to attempt the Imja. We were desperate to not have wasted our time. Pride had meant that I simply didn't want to sacrifice all the research. The flip side was that pride wanted me to push on to live what was left of the dream and finish the next page of the book so to speak.

A silence had covered our party someone had to speak and break the uncomfortable edge.

"Dave I think this changes the whole thing. Lets just us three go to the bar across the way and you and Martyn can sink a few. Leaving this room, these walls, might offer some resolution. Getting away might just put us in the frame, you know put focus on it, we can even take the money from the expedition kitty."

"Yeah, why the fuck not", Dave responded looking over at Martyn.

Picking up his hat and glasses from the table Martyn, still sullen. Stood and made tracks towards the doorway,

"I could do with a session."

The pub was quiet. It was only early and yet due the rain that had been falling for hours darkness was upon us. As we walked across the echoing floorboards all but few of the seats were vacant. Those taken were occupied by a couple of lads from the USA sat talking about the girls they had slept with whilst on a year out tour of the orient. The Sherpas looked on in disarray. As the bleached hairdo Casanovas compiled a stub by stud account of the best lays in the world. However banal the conversation it was a change to the stresses of the expedition and we soon joined in. How long ago was it since we'd made love? How young were we when we lost our virginity? Breasts or Bottoms, legs or lips? The conversation slipped into the gutter. Conversations often held in the changing rooms and men's clubs around the world. That's where it stayed. It was a relief. A filthy diversion but as the beer slipped down the necks of this ragtag bunch of travellers. We smiled. The world settled. Stresses levelled and with a clearout thought process we were able to sit once again and talk about our goals.

"I'm upset obviously but I don't know about you I don't want these boys to put themselves in danger just for us. Even the sight of us walking past might have been enough for the guards to question us or send us down the hillside and on the next plane back to Kathmandu and that was disappointing enough." I spoke honest.

"Perhaps its best that we walk back down to the check point just outside the National Park," downing his pint, Dave then continued. "It's for the best I guess, we could come back in a few years and get the official permit and all that." He spoke the truth, we both did.

"Yeah, I don't feel happy here, I just want to get on the bloody river." Martyn spoke slowly. His voice slow and deliberate was the whole truth and everything was honest.

As the hours passed our conversation never returned to the river or our predicament. We just enjoyed the jukebox. Shiva walked into the bar just before closing. He was alone and shivering with the wet shirt sticking to his body.

"Hi boys," he waved. Dave had already seen him walk into the bar and was busy buying Shiva a Beer.

"Here Shiva, drink this," Dave handed over the golden pint and whilst patting Shiva on the back continued. "It's ok, we don't want the boys, we don't want you to be in danger...Just tell em thanks but we gonna walk down in the morning."

"O boy that is ok, I know what it means to you, your expedition..."Shiva was smiling, relieved that we had done what he hoped for.

11
Break My Heart

The what, why and where have you been. The journey, the life and the time to be seen. Does it reflect the outer or the inner self or the truth and the death and the use of life? The puppet strings pulled from on high. Snipping and cutting away we would fall in a heap. The puppet master is in control. Mannequins must stand-alone before the security of the master can be detached.

We aren't crazy, we aren't seeking thrills, we just want the truth.
Doug Ammons

I don't remember going back to the lodge and I doubt neither Dave nor Martyn woke throughout the night for they had consumed a few beers. As dawn broke, heavy clouds hung in the air and through every drink of tea I felt sad. It was all over. We had made a sacrifice to change the expedition's aims just as our porters and friends were willing to sacrifice themselves for us.

The few days in Namche had been long and hard and now as Shiva rounded up the porters it was all change again. All the chaos and emotional stress was fading. We were to uproot from our base and return down the path we had walked up day earlier. The time that had progressed had changed us all.

The market place, the stupa would be only memories of a time spent within the kingdom in the sky. Between each mouthful of tea I found myself gazing towards the sky then back the stupa, how much I had received from it. Perhaps philosophically what I gained from Buddha in his actions, high on, was the understanding the sacrifice of putting on the river lower down. Through the bleakness a large Helicopter split the cloud base as its rotor arms spun slowly. The metal beast settled on the market, it wasn't an easy landing and I doubt that the pilot had done too many descents.

As I looked on, a small group of Sherpa men carried a black body bag into the hold. It was just another casualty of the mountain. It was a quick event, simple. No hassle was made, any stresses were voided; the Sherpa men and women just took this death as a periodic event. Man was not meant to challenge the mountain, going up or down. His life passed by with no obituary and no memorial. Then the body was gone.

As rain lashed on the window I couldn't help but think that the weather had come from the heart of The Mountain. The tears came for the dead. Stream of grief from Everest. It came for the disappointments that turns people back from the goal. Sleepy and clumsy Dave set up his video camera in the corner of the room. Flicking on the record switch I spoke to the video diary. I was easier to talk about this place than to write in my diary.

"After all the trouble with the army and the officials. All the influences of the Maoists... we have little choice but to move down. It is disappointing, true...but we are just changing our plans. We aren't going home in one of those black zip bags. That's about it."

I sat in silence, my hands were cupped together as I looked down to the floor. The record button was till on. Saying nothing told more about the events of the last few days than actually reeling off every word I could utter. It was my own memorial to those that will never see the green lush fields of home again. They will not see or know how people grieve. Adventure sport again is selfish.

Our porters dressed in plastic sheets shielding them from the rain lift the heavy loaded kayaks onto their backs. Slowly they descend. Porters are often very slow, they have so much weight to carry and now, what with the wet ground they must take extra care. The once dry and dusty streets the pathways that held so much hope days ago have turned into slippery sliding downward rivers of mud. The flip-flops and trainers are of no help. Its like walking on an ice treadmill, with a decline. It's hard to keep in control and even harder stopping.

For my part I'm dressed in my kayaking kit. Latex cuts into my neck from my dry top whilst in conjunction with my high waist waterproof trousers I am stopped from getting soaked to the skin. Martyn is dressed similarly, donning a walking cagoule over his thermal sweater but Dave has decided that just to wear his shorts and an old vest is the best method. I guess his clothes could have done with a wash. He could dry them later I suppose. Shiva still wearing his jeans holds a plastic sheet over his head and has wrapped it around his rucksack to protect the posters he has purchased, these are tucked inside and no doubt show images of the gods, of paradise.

The sombre walk down the river is silent. I don't want to speak, not least be spoken to. Cutting across the Dudh Kosi gorge the once bright prayer flags hang limp dragged down with the weight of water. Droplets heavily fall into the already swollen river. In the last few days the river has risen. With more volume the river is likely to be a lot more powerful. No longer is it a rock-infested ditch. The rocks, after such floods, hidden, the river encompassing all that it passes.

Violent and fast the river kept catching the corner of my eye. I didn't want to look at it. I didn't want to see what it held. It was hard to turn away. I had to. I didn't want to see what had taken all my emotions. When, unaccustomed to romance, a love affair ends that's how it was. I didn't want to look my lover, my ex-lover in the eye. I wanted to remember the good times not the heartbreak. I would do anything to crawl back to the good times. That is how it felt. The Dudh Kosi was breaking my heart.

After the steep descent into the gorge floor we were back again on the main trade and tourist route back to Lukla. It was desolately cold and like Dante's purgatory no place to be. No place to remember. At about 2775 meters we settled into the last lodge within the National Park. Dave shivered into his jacket and warmed himself by the fire.

Although it was cold, inside other guests sat looking at the steaming bowls of soup. With such heavy rain they would not want to continue upwards willing to sit out the storm without contentment. After ordering tea and hanging our wet clothes in front of the fire we disguised our kayaks in the back room. Covering them with blankets and crates of soda and boxes of chocolate. Our porters and Shiva would sleep here. No one wanted to stir any concern from the National Park checkpoint just over the bridge. They were just as likely to ask us to return to Lukla and fly back home. We spoke little that night. Hoping that in the morning we would be free to get on the river, finally able to paddle on the river from Everest.

Time passed slowly like the wet family holidays in the leaky caravan perched on the sea cliffs. Going out to the toilet was worse than peeing in the bucket on those caravan holidays. The toilet was across the path from the lodge, this meant that you had to be sure you really wanted to go and be ready for the onslaught of rain as it flooded the drains and open hole in the ground. One slip and that would be it, urine and excrement would run from the shoes. Such was the unpleasantness at the best of times and a cause for suicidal tendencies or murder among the cramped atmosphere of the expedition. We were after all sharing a triple bed, we could smell each other, feel each other scratch. A strong constitution and a pride in loosing personal space were important to keep the harmony.

During the night, where sporadic sleep grasped at our dreams I felt Dave wince in pain. Martyn was snoring and oblivious.

"You alright mate." I whispered to my left.

"Its just a head ache I guess."

"I've some water in the bottle on the window if you want."

"Thanks." And then I was off again to sleep.

The morning came all too soon. I had not gathered all the sleep I knew I needed. I was beaten and wanted a strong coffee. Although it's not possible. I have to reach for flask of tea when I first wandered into the haphazard dining room. Uncouth and selfish I rested my stocking feet against the still warm fire. Today was the day that all the training would come out in the real world.

Dave sat on the stones outside the lodge, it was no longer raining and between each drag from his cigarette he swallowed painkillers.

"You ok." I asked with a certain hesitation.

"I am screwed. I can hear from this ear," he pointed to his left ear with his hand, he was still holding the lit cigarette between his thumb and index finger. "But my right ear only has some hearing left. It fucking kills, you got any morphine in your bag?"

"Dunno Dave, I've got Valium and don't know what else."

"Could I 'ave 'em. I think they will help me sleep later, think it's a bloody ear infection, I keep getting puss and blood leaking out."

"Sure, take the tablets and let's just get on the river. If you want?"

12
Good Boy, Well Done

Frail life, torch light they arrived as we tried to sleep. A restless sleep full of demons of the night, please tell how did I get to this? How is it that I am curled on the rough wooden sleeping platform ready for the rest of my life? Fits of panic wake me. Exhausted bones ache for the slumber of a real bed. Adventure is suffering.

After all that had gone before, all that was to come, the river was a baptism. As I launched into the water. It's cool essence released from the high glaciers splashed on my chin and forehead. The idle drops cleansed me. I tasted the water of the Himalayas, the tears of Everest slipped down my lips.

Moving forward so few people had put strokes on this river. It was a privilege to be sat on the Dudh Kosi with only a few inches of the kayak between the water and my body.

Although I should have been focused on the river I could not but reminisce. In the first stroke all that had gone before, all that had influenced my reasons to come to Nepal collided in my mind. What seemed like decades ago, which was in fact just 3 years previous, I'd lit the blue touch paper on the adventurous fire in my belly. Late in September 2000 the concrete airport of Kathmandu was a new sight, full for strange images and sounds that have now become the everyday pleasures for me. I remember marvelling at the lofty peaks as I flew across from Bangladesh.

With a precise misscalculation, it seemed to my naïve eyes, the no doubt skilled pilot allowed the plane to descend on this make shift yet age-old permanent runway in Kathmandu. I was, it seemed in Nepal. Knowing that the touts and hawkers joined with the common thief just outside the terminal building. A friend who had been to Nepal before once said that they were the living human counter-part of bees around the honey pot.

Nestled in the corner of the arrivals lounge is a pre paid taxi counter. It is designed for safety, to safe the blushes of the unaccustomed traveller. It is pre paid in as much as 'give me the money before I show you the goods'. To this day I remember paying a small man behind the counter as a saffron robed monk nodded. A coincidence but I felt happy that he acknowledged my plight. It seemed aeons before the small taxi van appeared around the corner. With a flash of the US dollar my kayak, paddle and rucksack were forced into the little van and we were off down unknown streets.

I remember acting with hesitation as I rattled around the narrow streets on the way to the Hotel in Thamel. I remember eating Dhal Bhat for the first time and I remembered the 1st real Expedition River I did in Nepal. It was the ' Marsy' of the Annurpurna Massif with two friends, Hannah and Chris. I remember learning how to reserve energy and use minimal strokes to guide the kayak across and down the river. How to take chances with the river then assesses the conditions for whatever the probable outcome may be. When a risk could be calculated and when it was foolish to push on.

The ever-present danger of the river is often pushed into my mind. Never more concrete than from this early trip. On one such occasion I remember being waved over by two Nepali farmers as they, in broken English, told how a young farm hand had fallen into the river earlier in the day. They wanted to know if we could find him. It was a deathly environment. Throughout the trip the dark shadow of the reaper followed down stream. As the days passed we saw a small memorial funeral pyre on the side of the silt filled river. They had given up hope of finding him alive. The river had taken yet another life.

I was a quick learner and within 6 weeks I undertook a solo 1st descent on a river called the Budhi Ganga in the far 'wild' west of Nepal. It was hotspot for Maoist activity. I remembered how I was half-starved and concerned how I would ever get back to Kathmandu. Would the Maoists attack me? Would the river kill me? The true sense of adventure I felt on that day has never left me. I've never let it. The spirit drives me on.

Then I was off with the flow; the waves of the Dudh Kosi were powerful, the river playful in the extreme. It wasn't easy. That was not the point. Mostly the river was a succession of lethal hydraulics and large waves. If the river became too difficult Martyn would get out and walk down the river bank. Dave and myself pushed on alone. Headlong into the forever-falling horizon line that disappeared for view. Periodically we waited in the slack water below the rapids for Martyn to catch us up as he struggled to walk over the large boulders with his kayak on his shoulder. The porters had made it look so easy and looking on I was sure that Martyn would use less energy if he were to launch back into the river. We dare not speak to each other, nothing could diffuse from the intense concentration that we needed to find our way down the rapids. Running the river was a shear application of skill, a deafness to the outside world. The intensity of the surroundings threatened to engulf our kayaks.

Around each blind corner the landscape never gave up. It never rested. Boulders smooth by the ravages of time had become scattered around, interwoven, by the broken ice dams of the glacial lake outburst floods that happen periodically ripping the riverbed to shreds. The destruction caused was on apocalyptic proportions as if some giant mythic beast had become angry. As a child kicks an empty drinks can down the street or the drunk smashed his glass bottle against the wall. It was as such that the beast seemed to have laid waste to the Dudh Kosi.

The Dudh Kosi, named from the Hindi for milk river, carried slit and sediment down towards the mouth of the Indian plains, the Bay of Bengal. Our red and yellow kayaks, brightly coloured, stood out on this aquatic highway. Though we stood out our path was integrated to the river. However much we tried to escape we were part of it. Our journey, this wanderlust, had become a slave to the river. As the isolation and remoteness persisted I became a slave to the desire, to the aim of completion. It had taken so much of me. I wanted to give my new mistress all my soul. She could have it all so long that I lived, so long that I could retell the tale with pleasure. She was a dominatrix. They always are, these 'man-eaters', we cannot avoid the siren call.

This was the first time all three of us had run a river together, a kink appeared in our self-contained unit. Dave and myself would tackle the entire river provided we could see an escape line at the bottom, or maybe restful slack water half way down a succession of rapids. Martyn on the other had wanted to 'scout the river'. He wanted to see the whole map of the river before he continued. When we did this and took time over scouting and looking at lines Martyn would walk with his kayak. It seemed that he had already made his mind up and would obviously not like what he saw. He could hamper himself. Put him in undue danger. When on the river he often took the lines next to the banks, these were rock sieves viscously undercut just waiting to trap kayakers. As we paddled hard down the main lines of the river Dave would often shout to me. Feeling unsure of Martyn.

"Daz, he's putting himself in danger, we cannot be as slow with him, it's gonna be trouble," it was hard to hear his voice amidst the noise of the rapids but I tried to understand.

"He's freaked Dave, I know he can do it, leave it with me."

As Martyn rejoined the river again I could see how unsteady he was, how nervous he seemed, how robotic his actions. His normal fluidity had gone. For a world class paddler the mind game of expedition paddling just wasn't evident.

"Look Martyn, it's dangerous you out on the flanks all alone, you need to commit to the river." I spoke calmly, I wanted to boost his esteem.

"I know just let me settle in, don't rush me..." Martyn verged on anger with me, as if I'd put him in this situation.

It was a psychological minefield. He was a confident and able down river racing paddler. But the isolation and exposure was getting to him. He was beyond assistance. It is just one of these perils of expedition kayaking that you have to get on and just do it. If you thought about the consequences long enough then even I admit I'd never run the rivers I do.

With each turn in the river Martyn would ask about what was to come, what was coming up. Like I knew? Like Dave knew? None of us had been on this river before and even if we had I doubt I could remember. It was a personal descent into the unknown.

With every dropping twist and turn in the river the power and severity increased. The more we cut deep into the river the more technical and more life threatening the moves became. Just as the trail leads back to the river and trekkers can see the show. As the horizon drops we expect the fall that we had see on the way up. We had looked for routes when we passed on our way to Namche.

In order not to get swept away off the fall without cause we had no choice but to take the time to scout and look at the colossal hydraulic cascade. Our porters had caught up and were ready to carry the equipment around the madness.

"Hold on lads, I've seen a line." Dave thrust the video camera into my hand and walked towards his boat. Minutes passed and Dave had yet to set off.

The roar was immense and shouting to Dave, to ask if he was ok, would have been of little help.

Slowly and precise, the red of Dave's boat slipped past the smooth corner of the river. He was on line and with a quick stroke we saw him launch off the fall. Momentary he was airborne. He had cleared the drop. Landing softly in the aerated water he gave a quick thumbs up before paddling to the side.

It was my turn, my heart wanted so much to escape from my chest cavity. My hands were shaking. Even though Dave had made the move look smooth I didn't think I could. Dave sat higher in the water than I did. He floated on the waterline where my technique meant that I had to use the flow of the water, the undercurrents helped.

Walking back to my boat, I looked at the fall once again. The move was quite simple it required a slow descent to the lip and then a few quick strokes to clip the rock ledge this would send the kayak free from the hydraulic below. Launching off from the bank I knew what to do. I had memorised the ideal places to put my paddle and the ideal place to sprint for the lip. Breathing smoothly. I had to lowers my heart rate. The water took control and I was off. I wanted to paddle over to the right of the shoot that would give me the clearance. I put in a turning stroke but it wasn't enough. I was set for the midstream. Suddenly, without any thought I turned and paddled hard to the lip. I wanted to go with the flow, zen like. I wanted to go deep into the fall. That way I hoped that the undercurrents would kick me free. A tight stoke was made and I felt the river submerge me. Water shot down my back. The boat was unstable. I had to keep it upright. A flip in this water would put me in trouble. My hips held the boat tight. Then for a single moment it went dark. Silent and without motion.

I tried to breathe but was under water. My lungs would ache for air if I were to stay in this liquid prison. Light appeared on my right and I could feel the nose of the kayak begin to surface. I pulled hard with my paddle and with a few strokes sprinted. Then I was free. I had made the fall. I had no choice but to be reactive to the situation. But I had made it.

"That's it lads, I'm gonna walk this one, we have no dead hero's." With that Martyn reached for his boat and paddle and chose to portage the drop and the next rapid.

Phakding at 2652 meters was soon reached and we had already classed this village as a resting-place. After all we had left food and some gear in one of the lodges on the way up. At Phakding Bridge we pulled out of the river, the first day over. Elated we waited for the porters to find us. They could carry the equipment to the lodge. The sun burned down on us, drying us and warming throughout. Trekkers looked on in amazement as we sat down on the bridge supports. We were famous among the tourists and on more than one occasion we had to pose for photos. These were followed by the questions.

"Were you going?"

"India!"

"Where have you come from?"

"Namche."

"You're joking."

"No."

"Good luck."

"Thanks."

The questions were tedious and did little to ease our thoughts. Then running over the bridge a friendly sight.

"Hey guys, you crazy fools." It was the pilot from Namche, his American twang booming over the sound of the river.

"Hey you ok, what you doing down here now?"

"I'm off back to Lukla, should fly in the morning, but you are nuts. It's crazy, this river is nuts." Laughing he smiled and wandered off down towards Lukla before, in a few hours, he would be eating a meal in a real restaurant with the disorder of Kathmandu around.

13
Drug Pusher

Around and around we avoid the hardest route, life why take the easy way? Worth doing and worth the effort, but is it? How hard do you push the body and the soul? The pleasure of the path of resistance has little wear. More genuine more authentic to the truth. Footsteps marked in the dust and spider webs are swept across the palace entrance. No one dare enter since who knows what will be found?

"Shiva, how can we get some drugs?" Dave spoke of the pharmaceutical requirements that would ease the ear infection. The pain was a constant reminder, a mute testimony to the ravages of expedition living. Everyone felt it, some more that others.

"I'm having trouble with my chest, can you help?" Martyn piped up, coughing and croaking. He was squinting against the early morning sun. Such a posture didn't help his already weathered appearance. Eyes glazed colourless and withdrawn he showed no hope and no joy. Balls of green semi-solid liquid arched from his throat when he coughed spitting phlegm to the floor.

"For your troubles I can go to the rescue medical station, it is a few hours walk away, you just get on the river to Ghat. Then you have to walk for a few hours. I will see you tonight, just aim for the last lodge…in the village, o, forget the name… sorry…"

"How will we find you… we're in the bloody Solu Khumbu?" I hated to ask but I didn't want to walk the wrong way. Without a map we had no reference for distance. We couldn't pace our walk, not knowing when to rest. We just had to walk until we stopped, until the warm glow of the lodge and Shiva could be seen. A beacon of solace that would without a doubt occupy every thought on the long march into the night.

"Don't worry I will speak with the local guides and the farmers. I will tell the porters. It's on the trade route to Jiri. I think they will know the village, just follow them."

Then he was gone and walking quickly down the path towards Lukla. There it forks diverting to Jiri in the south. The Jiri path is less trodden, harsher on the feet. It sees few western feet but the supply-chain; basket-backed heavily laden porters use the track daily. Resting points are abundant, scattered periodically between the rugged ancient and unkempt mani walls where the ashes of fires used as the porters heat up lentils and rice before stopping for the night. As we waved towards Shiva, all we could do was get back on the river. It was the quickest way down. All we could hope was that the medical station held the medicine for Dave and Martyn.

Explosive waves rocked the boats from left to right. It sure as hell woke us from the previous night's comfort. Walking from Ghat as we would later in the day was now not of concern to us. The cold river was unrelenting. It never gave up. The water never rested. In its fury it focused the mind. Our attention was diverted from daydreaming and sightseeing onto what was happening at that precise moment. It made our world small unifying our thought process as a group into as linear pattern. All that mattered was how we managed to navigate our small plastic boats down the river. We were equally alone with our own perspectives and aims.

The slack pools were getting smaller. Harder and harder the rapids hit home in quick succession. Like the automatic tennis ball-serving machine. Pushed against the net we had to act fast if we wanted to survive. Waves caused obstructions, let alone the glaring sun and the steep descent. Vision was minimal or none existent at times. Each wave, each rock, each one of the falls in the river double backed onto the next. I tried to make it a survival tendency accepting fate and what the fury had to give. The linear thoughts were reactive. Nothing else would do. Reactions were the only way to survive. Leading sections wasn't easy for anyone but some body had to be in the inaugural position. Out alone at the front meant pioneering the route. This made choices imperative. One missed stroke, one missed judgement and that would be the end. Those following could see where the mistake was made. They would be able to react. Out at the front you had to be firm in running the rapid. Confidence and skill were not enough. A self-righteous arrogance had to seep slowly from the psyche.

Taking it in turns Dave would leap frog to the front. We would sandwich Martyn into the group. It was a safety device. At times even this was not enough and he would paddle to the side again, lifting his kayak he would walk.

"Martyn, hold on," Dave shouted above the roar of the river.

"I'm not up for it, Dave just leave it."

"Ok, walk man, but could you get some video footage?" Dave thrust the small video camera into his hand. "Look we will wait for you to get down this section. It's easy to use, just wait for us to paddle to the bottom of the 1st drop then pack the camera away, we will see you in a bit."

Following Dave I sprinted for the main flow. A hydraulic ramp, a curling wave pushed against the back of my boat. I was off guard and over balancing; I could not find a place to balance mid-flow. I was unable to stay stable and online. Then it was wet. I could no longer feel air on my face. I could not recall how I had tipped. My paddle, snagged on the water, made heavy by the pressure. It became a dead weight in my already tired arms. Rocks rolled underneath on the riverbed. I could hear them rumble against the hiss of the silt that echoed in my ears. I had to right my kayak quickly and without hesitation. Instinctively I had to execute an Eskimo roll before my lungs began to inhale and take on water. Less than a second passed. It felt like an eternity before I could see again. I could breath again although drawing deep breaths meant that I swallowed water when I impacted head long with the giant turbulent waves. Getting sufficient air into my lungs required that I tilt my head to one side so that all the water went on my side. True, this motion lost visibility whilst my head was turned but I regained air.

As the waves crashed into my kayak and chest I had to plan a route down river. I had lost Dave in all the foaming chaos. Only his helmet could be seen in the distance. Further down the river, he was at least upright. I had lost my mental map, I didn't know where I was on the river. All I could do was hope that the strokes I made would release me from any danger, away from a watery grave.

Recording the action Martyn held the camera still. The digital zoom focused in on the upturned kayak. The frames seeing what I never could. Only the camera knew exactly what was happening. No time to think. Getting down the river was my only concern. I needed the sanctity of the flat relaxed water I could see on the right, just 600 yards below.

Elated my heart rate eased. It had been fun, heart pounding scary and at the edge of reason. The relief of making it that's what it's all about.

"Top section Daz." Dave shouted.

"Sweet."

"What you say, I'm still deaf."

"IT WAS GREAT, A CLASS 5 I QUESS...THE LIMIT."

"Yeah a 5, possibly harder a 5plus."

"THAT'S THE HARDEST RAPID I'VE EVER RUN ON SIGHT. BRILLIANT."

Martyn joined us again and as the rapids eased we all became more relaxed. Although I was the must unfit and the most overweight among us it seemed that I was the only one without any serious problems.

As we crawled from the river and up the steep incline to

Ghat, where the porters sat on the stones that flanked the river waiting, I was the only one that didn't need to rest. The ascent took no effort from me yet the others were struggling. Dave's ear infection was obvious, yellow liquid seeped from his ears and once in a while blood pooled in the lower ear. Martyn wheezed and coughed spitting phlegm out to the side of his mouth. Occasionally this would stall in its flight turned by the wind it would dribble down his beard before he could wipe it clean with his hand.

Lunch was weak tasteless and dull noodle soup from the small stall frequented by the porters and farmers at the end of the village. As we ate from the basic foodstuff outside our porters waited and guarded our kayaking equipment. On the fence at the far side of the track we had put all our wet kit to dry. The helmets and paddles were of great interest to all that passed, both young and old picked up the articles of interest. Dirty juvenile faces smiled and danced around under the helmets. Even though they were ergonomically shaped some how the youngsters always put them on backwards. As if picking up a precious jewel they fingered the fabric of our paddles.

"Plastik, plastik," one of our porters was trying his hand at passing his knowledge on about the sport to all that would listen. He was young and keen. We guessed that although the ravages of hard work had worn his skin his eyes and smile were younger. He was a young man trapped inside the working organism, the skin and bones, damaged by age. Talking in Nepali we could only make out the English words he could find no comparison for.

"Rafting," the chatter would grow faster and without breath
"Chatra." We would hear him say. It was true that we were off to Chatra, not far from the Indian border, but that was not today, it was not what we had our mind set on.

Thinking one day at a time, one step at a time, the walk to meet Shiva was the only thing I could think of. Each step was a step towards bedtime. The peace that dreams can bring where the anticipation and the stress could just fade into the unconscious. Freud would have a field day with that one. How would he interpret the want to regress into dreams as escape?

Monotony and the marching of time, each footstep closer is one further from the starting point and one closer to the end. Dusty paths cut deep into the hills as footsteps let tiny impressions in the soil. Fatigue had set in as the path lead way from the forked crossing at Lukla. Miles upon miles of dense forest hung on the valley walls as a slim dusty trail channelled finally towards the distant clouds. Side streams joined the impossible falling chasm of the Dudh Kosi with regularity. Those on foot, which was all there ever was in this region, had no choice but to trek away from our aim until we could find a suitable crossing point. It was demoralising and forced us passed exhaustion. We had kayaked hard pushing our personal limits all morning. At home that would have been it for the day, content with what we had done. Alas the river would not let us rest. We had to walk. As the hours ticked past and light began to fade all the mystery and romance of the surroundings were of little interest, the postcard views were lost on me. "Wish You Were Here". I would not even wish that for my worst enemy. I know that few had walked this path but I did not want to be this tired. I just wanted to rest, although I knew that the walk would be continuous. Tedious at best this trail would be our home for the next few days until we could join the river again. Deep in the gorge below the river was indeed truly not navigable flowing violently hundred of meters down reverberating against the rocks the forested walls were unable to silence the acoustic hell. From high up we could make out individual features of the river with waves and waterfalls that would kill anyone who attempted to conquer them.

Our porters kept good time. Walking slowly they would

stop only to reorganise the heavy loads. Pointing skyward the stern of the kayaks often caught on overhanging branches forcing the porters to curl over tightly. Forcing them to look like a psychedelic snail. On steep descents the nose of the boats would bounce on the rocky steps or click hard into the heels of the carries. Weighing over 40 kg the loads were not the heaviest the guys had carried but they were perhaps the most unwieldy and cumbersome.

Dusk fell slowly on the clear night, but the whole area was already dim. The canopy of trees and the shadow of the surrounding foothills kept sunny crimson haze from barely touching the pathway. Hoping for Shiva to show up too tired to continue we were all suffering, not our usual joyous selves.

Stalling to rest a while, I perched on a small purpose made porter rest stand. The stones rounded and smooth from the years of buttock erosion I took a drink from my stained and chipped water bottle.

"Hey Dave, look at this porter, a footie fan."

"No chance, that's an Arsenal top...."

Dave turned to the resting porter next to us. His old bright yellow Arsenal football top stained red. On his back a worn and tired basket held yak meat. Fresh, the unsealed joints glistened with blood open to grime and insects.

"Namaste," Dave looked over at the young lad.

"Are...you Elglish...I Nepal...Hi,"

"Hi, me Dave. You have meat, masu, for sale?"

"Masu, *pasa, apke pas...ha*".

Dave and this remote door to door butcher discussed at length the purchase of meat in local dialect. The financial business of such a transaction were lost on me and I doubt the translation opened any conversation of length. Our own porters rested the kayaks against a small wall before walking over. Between smiles and broken syntax a large rusty knife was produced. Cutting away the fat a few kilos of meat was handed over to Dave. Dripping in blood he quickly stuffed the parcel it into the back of his kayak. With the formalities of payment done we were once again on the trail.

"Well that's supper lads, even got some extra for the porters and the didi when she cooks tonight. Speaking of which I think it would be a good idea if we got out our head torches. Its gonna be black in a while, past dark, no street lights and I cannot see any villages." This gesture would have been most generous to the house for which we would be staying. The 'didi', woman of the house, would without a doubt make a spicy meat curry for anyone who wanted to indulge.

"It's great being a veggie". I saw the light-hearted thought that Dave had made to boost morale. "Bet you could do with a beer as well, lets just hope it's not long before we get to Shiva. That Rice and Lentil surprise will be so nice."

"And a cuppa, I could murder a cuppa," Martyn piped up.

"The quicker we walk now the quicker we will get to the lodge, you set Dave? You set Martyn? And let us not forget the dancing girls!"

One by one our torchlight rounded the bend with the thought of food speeding our tracks into the indefinite fading horizon of the night.

14
One Step At A Time

Screaming and kicking the naked flesh escapes from the bleeding womb of the mother. The life one cannot spy into the future and what it is to behold. Questions draw as things get answered with bias. Is the answer that to be happy is to be alone, to venture on your own spirit to your own Shangri-La, the mystic religion of the East answers.

Misty breath escaped into the early morning chill. It had been a night of little sleep. However exhausted my mind just wouldn't rest. I was the first to leave the lodge. Sitting on the damp rocks the moisture seeped through my shorts. I struggled to know if the mist would blow away or if we were sat in the cloud line. I knew that the dampness of the cotton wool cartoon clouds would soak the skin and clothes. From talking to porters before retiring to bed a blasé estimate was that we had about two more days on the trail.

I was keen to push on and finish the walk. I had come to Nepal to kayak and found this trek a chore. On the flip side I wanted to be alone with my thoughts and the comfort of my nylon sleeping bag. I also knew that people pay through the nose for a trekking holiday and the simple pleasure of strolling through the foothills of the Himalayas. Perhaps I should have been joyous. It was the bags under my eyes that made me think like this. I'm sure it was!

Again and again the circus of three kayakers, and a drinking buddy from Dave's past would be followed by the plastic turtle backed porters. When the sun came out not long into the foot march down hill the surroundings could been seen in all the majesty and heavenly glory. Clouds parting only then would I be able to smile.

As time passed the steady pace of feet against the earth became meditative. I was settled with the adventure. Hand made homes open to the elements formed small hamlets hugging close to the path. Women dressed in colourful saris cluttered unbolted doorways. Ripped and dirty through the ravages of time the fabric shielded natural beauty as it prevailed on the smooth skinned child brides.

The idle chatter would cease as we walked by. Half-nervous with us around all females, from the nimble to the aged, would scuttle into the kitchen to avoid meeting us. Men were conspicuous in the absence. Only the elderly and the children of the male gender could be seen. With every village, every house the usual carefree attitude of Nepalese hospitality was fading.

For hours I'd noted Hindi styled writing on the walls and houses that littered the path. It adorned the outposts of the villages and was, at times, echoed in the dirt. Red marks blotted the landscape like the leaky ink from an over used felt marker pen

"Shiva, what is all the stuff, all the graffiti?"

"Dasss, sshh, it's Maoist...that all you need to know..."

Averting from my gaze, I knew that he didn't want to discuss it. I could figure the rest my self. The slogans were a form of Maoist propaganda. Political advertising to the uneducated rural masses; in a country where adult literacy is only about 35% for the whole nation every thing was open to misunderstanding and slander.

"Ok Shiva, I get it...but why are they shy up here, not as 'smiley' as the other villages." I tried to explain how emotionally cold I felt the villages were.

"It is Maoist, they come and want money, if not...whack... they will beat the family or rob them or worse...it is... they ask a percentage from the families." His voice was hushed and although directed towards my questions he looked around to see who could hear. "That is why they say all of rural Nepal supports them....they are bullied into it...but the army and police also charge for protection...they cannot win."

His conversation tailed off as Dave approached.

The next few minutes we walked in silence. With the brief insight into the hill politics I suddenly noticed the occurrence of the painted socialist logos painted on some of the houses. The hammer and sickle look out of place, disturbing the ambience of the surrounding that in such a small time since breakfast, I had been growing to love. The manifesto of Marx seemed to conflict with a rural pace of life that was as old as the hills and although ancient in ideology the feudal system that it represented worked well. It was only with the growth of the capitalist movement that the young Maoist ideology was fighting back harder and with more vigour.

"Boys, come here....it is getting to be secret...I have a suspicion that the Maoist spotters are watching us...we don't want to give to them...stop filming, hide the money they will want it all." Even up in Namche I had not seen Shiva so nervous. Now miles from any settlement it looked like we could get robbed blind.

Slowly we divided the equipment. All I carried was my camera and a few dollars. My shiney new SLR camera although bought for the trip would have to be the sacrifice if it meant we could keep the footage from the video that Dave had. I recalled the similar event in Num, years earlier and how we were lucky. As the years had progressed the Maoist cause had wanted more from its donors. Donations of over 100 pounds were not uncommonly received from tourists. This is not to say that the donors truly wanted to flourish the Maoists with gifts but it freed their ransom so to speak.

Our plan, if the situation changed and became threatening, was for us to first offer only ten American dollars each and see if they would settle for that. After all the American currency spoke volumes. It allowed the Maoist movement the ability to purchase weapons on the black import market. We all understood the implications of giving to the Maoist cause but how else were we to barter with them?

The deeper we walked into this Maoist heartland the more anxious we all became. Anxiousness shadowed all of us. We walked in silence alone in our thoughts. Each person we passed we saluted with 'Namaskar'. Holding our hands up in prayer, a little respect would go a long way. It was not the time to upset the apple cart, to dislodge the state and area rules. It was not the time to speak our minds. I, for one, had done that too much. I had to learn how to bite my tongue. It was best that I only saluted with my hands and a hushed inaudible 'hello-namaskar'. It was easy not to offend that way I guessed.

Rancid milk coagulated against the butter and salt of the Tibetan tea. Offered with pride it sat untouched on the greasy table. It was a beverage feared by many, the drink of legends. It had to be drunk. To leave it would have been disrespectful to our hosts. It was not the tea I wanted not the golden milk sweet delight that I loved Nepal for. I did want to gulp the tea down, it was just too much effort to chance more of the unknown.

Our hosts were of Tibetan origin and fought hard to keep their traditions and culture alive a few miles within Nepal. Ideally suited as a service stop for the number of porters this once nomadic family had made a home of mud and wood. Cluttered in the corner, next to the open fire and blackened pots, were the blankets and sleeping platforms. Boxes of trinkets were covered with rush matting. In a time of political turmoil and Maoist banditry it was of no benefit to show off charms however meagre the wealth seemed. A large bucket of water balanced precariously as a door wedge allowing a stream of light to flood the lodge. Prisms of dust were highlighted in the stream. Floating in the air, the steady breeze could not quite disperse the unsettled particles before it fell to the ground.

After tea and a token noodle soup whilst Dave cleaned the blood from his ear we got ready to walk again. The path was unforgiving with each crest and each bend I had to keep my mind active. It was easy to become a slave to the walk. I had to think of the people that would never see such sights. My Godson, on his christening a few years back, would not know of the diversity in the world. I had wanted to educate him. Wrapped the silver foil of expensive gift paper around a children's picture atlas and a bank balance. The former I hoped would fuel the young mans quest to travel. Like me I hoped he would see the world. The latter was a saving account to be used at age 18 for a flight around the world. Dreaming for the day when I would lift his back pack on to his teenage shoulders as side by side we would walk through the security check and visa posts boarding the plane to lands unknown. His parents, I still don't know if they think it a wise choice, have been friends most of my life. The semi-detached two-car life style was so far devoid from everything I knew. My life amused them. Was it that they dare not do what I do? Was I Peter Pan in the parental eyes avoiding the structures of the family and home life.

Steps still had to move us forward. Pounding our feet had to be lifted. Sweat clung in our hair as the intense heat of the day beat down. Occasionally landslides had destroyed the pathway forcing the trail to scramble on precarious ledges balanced by the improvised wedges of felled trees. From the ball of the foot to the heel the rhythm must be kept. Minor descents forced the knees to absorb the shock. Whilst the steep ascents required that the calf muscles were forced to work over time it was exhausting. Not wanting to rest each simple step required a grasp of air into the lungs. Weaving forever onward the trail was the master we had no choice but to keep drawn by its lines in order to reach a resting-place for the night.

Houses and villages were hesitantly scattered by long gaps of forest. How far was too far to walk, so that we would end up sleeping in the middle of the path, stranded between the villages? None of us knew. Our porters had walked this way most of their working lives but they could not time the walk. The loads slowed them and the landslides added to such delays.

The cloud line hung on the last peak around the final bend in the valley. We could not see the path as it wound its ever-changing course buried deep into the distance. Only then would we be able to get back on the river again. It would be a descent back to the aquatic life style that's all we knew about our sense of purpose.

From nowhere, out of the mist or appearing as phantoms, teenage Nepalese men would run up to meet us. Sporting trainers and jeans they carried little on their backs. These were not porters and in the heart of such wilderness what was their reason to be on the trail? Eyes pierced us, stopping us dead in our tracks. None spoke. Uncontrollably the rib cage and chest struggled to control my heart. Anxious thoughts over filled my mind and coagulated as the red blood of life running down my veins through my pulsing arteries I could feel my heart beat stronger than ever. As we walk further into certain terrorist homeland no official state control could help. Away from the army and the protection of the tourist trade one thing and one thing only existed as fact, the rebel Maoist forces control the region. Shiva says they are watching us. Their runners keep talking to Shiva, he knows.

"Lads, they are watching, we must be with the porters, we must take care," Shiva spoke soft as if telling the child off for a misdemeanour. He was serious, firm but understanding. Silence then overtook as we paced towards the nearest village, it was still light as the houses and small concrete school building came into view. As elsewhere in Nepal the children, dirty faced and bare footed, ran up the path to greet us. Calls of 'Namaste' followed as they chased after the plastic boats on the back of the porters. Pulling at our clothes they mithered for sweets and money, pens and pencils. It was harmless unlike the touts in Kathmandu. Unthreatening and playful we let them huddle around as Shiva wandered further into the village.

"Dave...Daasssss,...Marteeen...you and the porters wait... take a rest, I will find a place to stay." He shouted back. Seated at the feet of the children as they played we waited. Our porters, resting the boats against the walls and boulders separating the path from the fields of substance farming, joined us. On their haunches they chatted idle words among themselves. Occasionally the farmers would walk from the fields carrying basic tools covered in the heavy earthen soil. Pleasantries would be exchanged and those that didn't have to rush on home would sit and pass the time. I knew the conversation would be no different to the one I would have if I bumped into any tourist hikers.

"So hi, where have you come from?"

"Where are you going?"

"How long have you been on the trail?"

The questions were generic. Like the first day I went to university I remember everyone I saw asking the same bloody questions. I remember the spotty naïve faces portraying a self imposed importance. First year freshers would ask the questions with false interest, really just wanting to talk about themselves. Each question was leading but hollow.

"Hey man I'm Steve...and you are?...but my mates call me Thumper, it's a nick name...cool eh?" An awkward pause would hang in the air, I doubt that Steve, or indeed anyone else would have listened to my name since throughout the evenings of first meetings I would have to reiterate who I was. I also reminded people that I didn't know them. Even on the day I left university I didn't recall the name of the girl who sat at the front of the seminar room every second day.

In order to keep the conversation flowing somewhat I would pass on my name.

"Yea, Steve... I'm Daz."

"Cool man, I've just done four A levels, and you? I think this is gonna be a trip place to live…I'm from London this place is far out." I remember the conversation somehow but now in the passage of time I cannot recall what I said and I doubt Steve would remember. It was always the same, names and memories that fade into the façade of time.

Waiting in limbo for Shiva it was strange where the mind went. In the middle of the trek, away from it all with the pressure of the river and the arduous walk. With the Maoist movement in the area and the impending river in a few days the mind was on edge, just not knowing what would happen. Normal routine of the day to day in the UK was gone. It all fell away. Until as the minutes passed Shiva walked wearily back up the path.

"Is ok, follow me we have a small cottage to use, the family are going to cook and the children will sleep outside on the floor, outside with the porters. We have food from them, then sleep, it long way in the morning follow me." Collecting the plethora of equipment that we had scattered across the pathway we sloped off after Shiva. Down the alleyway towards the cottage, harvested ploughed fields flowed on terraced into the bank. Sanitation was minimal as the remnants of human or beast excrement and urine clung to the rocks and entwined with the dirt.

"The children will sleep on the rough mat just here". Shiva pointed to an area in the open courtyard. "You can have their beds…they will not mind." As the evening progressed through the grey smoke haze of the fire we tucked into the stable diet of rice and lentils. One at a time the children would gather up blankets and old clothes to make the bed on the floor suitable for the night. Tired we ate in peace wondering when would be suitable to retire to bed ourselves. Would it be rude to keep the host family up later then they would normally? How would we know?

"Boys I so sorry…this is not the place I wanted to stay,"

Shiva spoke quietly, his back to the family. Hiding his words he spoke only in English hoping that they would not understand. "Well boys...I have a friend who has a house in this village...we would have been welcome, but I tried to go. It is not to be, the Maoist have taken control of his home. They are living in it... It was just behind the path you were sat on. The Maoist...they have seen us, they know you are...but I think if they wanted money then they would have been to see us already. In the morning once we leave the village I think, I am sure," he thought carefully about his words, "then on the way to my village we will be safe...it time for us to go to bed now, time to rest long day."

Collecting up our thermal tops and hats we climbed the flimsy matchstick like ladder to the balcony bedroom. Walking out again minutes later to urinate in a suitable place away from the family home. The dark sky was covered with only stars away from the clouds that hung as rings around the foothills opposite. Crisp a chill would come in the night. I was pleased with the sleeping bag and the additional blankets on the beds. Sleep would come quick as in the morning the walk would be even more demanding, even more challenging.

15
The Bosom Of The Family

Many never understand the simplicity of the family. The ties of blood that the modern world dispenses are the love lost. Love gained from the fickle fate of promiscuity as it pulls away from the unit. Traditions are lost and black sheep hide in the shadows. Home Sweet home.

"I AM NOT A FUCKING MOUNTAIN GOAT." Swearing with frustration Martyn struggled with the climb up to Shiva's home village. If the walk had been in Britain experienced Mountain Leaders would have roped clients up and assisted with bracing devices to stop people falling. This was not the case as my foot wobbled on the smooth rock face. Wet the sandals offered no grip and strapped loosely as they were I could not feel the ground beneath. The climb was not made any easier by the paddles we were carrying. It was thought that we could help the porters this way. It was our paddle, we looked after it. If we broke it then it would be our own fault. On the river these paddles were the best tools in the world. But they made bad walking sticks and were too cumbersome and unwieldy to have on such a climb. We had but to reach the top as a tripod. The ravages of the days spent on the trek were coming to an end, but we were not quite settled yet.

More than the pace it was the heat and the intense stress of walking into the unknown. Pouring and overflowing the blood left the heart...returning back after the tour of the body too tired to go again...Home was just after the next corner...the next corner never comes.

Low beams and the vast number of people meant that we had no choice but the huddle squatting or with crossed legs as four generations of the family celebrated the turn of their elusive son. Even more special was the group of his friends from Britain. These men from afar were going to tackle the raging river below.

Our aim of the river was of no significance. We were just a break in their rural routine. At home the vacuum cleaner sucks up from the carpet and yet this dry mud floor, highlighted by white wash walls, seemed spotless. It was kept tidy with self-respect and pride, not just because of the guests but because of value and an intrinsic understanding of cleanliness. A water filled pit was cut into the ground and covered with solid square earthen slabs. It was a luxury, a basic but apt fridge. Large copper pots were displayed on thick wooden shelves above the fireplace. Below, women of all ages sat on haunches needing dough. Occasionally one or the other would sweep hair away from their face, away from the large golden nose rings.

It wasn't long before the dough was turned into thin bread called roti. Traditionally this was eaten with a milkey by product, the curd. As honoured guest we were served first. Thanking was not enough. To speak would have been of little concern. It was much more important that we devoured with relish and without looking greedy waited for more. The bread and curd was a simple meal that made me feel like a king.

To my right Shiva's Granddad looked into my eyes. We spoke no common tongue but producing the universal thumbs up followed by a smile I felt content. I felt pressure on my shoulder as he squeezed. His firm powerful fingers were non-threatening. It was a friendly bonding moment between generations and cultures. I lent over to pat him on his back. The patriarch had raised a fine family. Laughing, even though we had not spoken he held close body contact momentarily. Strangers in the night, I respected his family values and he, I'm not so sure, did he truly respect and understand what the tall white Englishman was doing? Wordless and silent a deep full bodied smiled lifted from my heart.

"Hey Dasss, my granddad, he likes you."

"Yea Shiva TELL HIM I THINK THE HOUSE ITS GOOD HE HAS A GOOD FAMILY".

"OK....". Shiva then spoken fast in Nepali whilst his family all looked at me. Laughing and clapping the whole room rejoiced. Laughter and smiles warmed both the room and the hearts resting in the bosom of the family. Values of blood and sweat were once again bounded together.

Throughout the night, as the chatter and food ran out I returned to the bedroom I had been offered. Even though the company was great and I would have loved to have stayed awake all night and pass the hours, to ask questions about real family life, it was not to be. Heavy, my eyes closed like the shutters of a shop at closing time. The daily route of the hill life I would cherish to learn more about it. About how life develops when the year is ruled by the seasons. For such learning I would have to wait until morning. I said thank you to the family before taking the short walk to the room we had been given. Firm handshakes with all took time. I suspected they didn't want me to leave.

I dragged my sleeping bag and mat from the pile of junk on the bed taking the time to look around the room, using the light from my fading torch. Old Hindu language newspapers were piled high on top of wooden boxes. The bare wooden floor, rough and untreated, was only covered in part by rush style covers. Candle wax droplets were on the walls and remaining floor space. Torn and aged photomontages dusty by time were nailed to the wall near the door. Granddads hoarding artefacts covered the walls. It was akin to the mess and hassle of a teenager's bedroom but with the distinct lack of 'girlie' photos. Opposite the door was a giant poster, a hammer and sickle logo of the socialist and communist party. Shiva's family was unexpected Maoist sympathisers?

Undressing quickly I wriggled into bed. I was getting

accustomed to the movement restriction of the tight bag as I pulled the hood tight over my head. My fleece jacket offered a sufficient pillow. Jerking suddenly I felt that I was falling out of bed, which was strange since I was laid out flat on the floor. I steadied my body and nestled into sleep.

It was deep unconscious slumber that I finally fell into. Although I had obviously been on edge before my eyes became heavy. I know that Dave and Martyn joined me to sleep in the room as when I got up in the morning they were fast asleep, but I don't remember them waking me.

"Morning boys...Tea," Shiva stood in the open doorway, how long he had been watching his friends as sleeping cherubs was unknown.

"Yeah Shiva, and tea and everything for the boys, give them a treat in bed."

"I know look." On the floor by his feet were three cups of pepper tea, he had read my mind.

"Hey Shiva, you got a fag," Dave still tight in his sleeping bag murmured.

"Sure, my man I will go get 'em."

Shiva scuttled down to the room below where his jacket hung against the door as Dave dug his way out of his sleeping bag.

"Hey Daz, Shiva told us last night after you went to sleep... well you know how his mother ain't here."

"Yeah, I just figured that she lived some place else."

"Naar, not the case. She died on that rock face that we walked over, the steep climb that Martyn hated. She slipped in Monsoon and lay dead at the start of the path."

"Wow, so who brought him up?"

"O, his Grandparents. Shiva then went to Kathmandu to earn some money for his family. I guess that was in the bag he gave them before we all went to bed."

"I think maybe we should do the same, leave them a gift."

"Yeah some rupees and if we have any spare kit."

"That sounds top, Dave you let me know what you think is right. I'm gonna get some air, have a slash and wait for more tea. My mouth is dry and I got a spinning head."

Throughout the 'Chow mien style' noodle breakfast we collected our belongings and got set to return to the river. In a few hours we would be back fighting with the Dudh Kosi. The walk would be over and Shiva would return to Kathmandu after spending a few more days with his family. He would fly back with our excess equipment. We no longer needed our duvet down jackets or our extra thermal tops and hats. Our waterproof dry trousers were also surplus and although damp from the last time we were on the river were stuffed into one of our dry bags. These were lashed with a fine rope onto the back of Shiva's rucksack so that he could carry them to the plane. The bag would then sit under the desk in the Drift office until we arrived back in Thamel Kathmandu to collect it.

A small plastic bag held sweets and some money, we left it behind on purpose. Telling Shiva it was a present for his kind family. They had not asked for money or gifts but now more than ever we felt, not from duty, to offer more back than we had received in kind. We left them without a word and headed for the river.

16
All Good Things

The drawing of the curtain and the stage fall silent. No encore is
offered. Just the one off solo show that's what we have. The show will
be different when someone else views it. The replay will never be as
good as the first setting. It's just a show for an audience of one.
None the less the players had worked for years in this adlib play.
Walk the boards and wait applause.

Turbulent waves cut down the river. Since we left it days ago
it had gained volume from the steams that joined. Rocks, the
once natural slalom, were deeply buried under the flow.
Restless angry surges were unsuspended in time. Rising from
the pit to the foaming peak was the only way to see down the
river. Each succession of waves left our route to chance. One
foul move and we would end up stuck in the massive
hydraulic ramps. These were at best hard to escape from and
at worst a holding zone to certain death.

Larger and consistently growing the river features awesome
and commanding. They failed to cease and hold back in slack
flat pools. Cutting fast to the bank Martyn beached his kayak
between two rocks and clambered out. Without a word he
began to walk dragging his kayak behind him on a rope.
Downstream the river continued its fierce pace, Dave and
myself were charging the river fighting with the rapids as
Martyn walked along side.

"Martyn, you've gotta get back on for your own sake, you
cannot walk the river, if that's the reason you might as well
walk back to the village. Catch up with Shiva then go back
home, it's not gonna get any easier." They were hard and
harsh words that Dave spoke over the noise of the roaring
river, when he was able to get close to the bank as the flow
stalled in a small smooth rapid.

"Look Martyn...you have two choices, get on and paddle or

go back, we cannot, simply cannot, carry on with you like this". I had to say what I felt. Martyn had to choose at this low point in his psyche he was a liability to both himself and the expedition.

Paddling slowly down the river we then waited for Martyn. His choice would change the pace of the trip. Without Martyn, however overwhelmed by the river he was, we had no reference point. The way Dave and myself ran rivers was viewed as mad and insane by some. We ran in a style call 'blue angel' stealth like. We trusted each other and allowed the leader to choose the safest line. We left two to three yards between one another. For the most part we ran the river in the main flow, main lining so to speak. However committing this was the safest in such violent water. Pushed up against the banks, where Martyn would paddle if he were in his boat, were sucking rock jams and siphons. The banks often undercut in addition forming deep caves to trap the unwitting in a watery casket. Missing a move here, although the water wasn't as powerful, would have lead to certain death, drowning by entrapment. The kayak pressing the body into the rocks or sucked forever down the plug hole vortex to the depth of the riverbed. It was a place that one could not be self rescued from and a place that those in the main flow could not see to offer assistance.

Robotic like paddle strokes propelled Martyn into the flow as he joined up with us. It seemed he'd chosen to give it a go. Was he being stubborn in not letting the river beat him down? Did he not want to loose face with his friends? Did he truly think he could deal with the river?

"I'm gonna try harder, I know I've let you down lets just crack it on...Dave, Daz lets go, sorry." We both nodded in unison and were off again into the main flow. Twisting our torso muscles and bracing the boats with our legs we were able to direct the plastic beasts in a smooth carving motion scooting a traverse across the flow to avoid the large boulders and foaming hydraulic traps. It was unrelenting activity, where we were only kept stable through the use of our paddles in the water. A simple stroke that beginners learn is the low brace, a stroke that can if used correctly cease the wobble factor. Adapted this stopped us from falling off balance and ending up falling upside down in the waves.

Constantly smacked in the face by the raw power of the waves made the heart race again. Pounding it was hard to balance and control such aerobic activity and emotions. The sweat of concentration and stress cannot fail to be washed away by the waves. As they smashed into our faces saturating our skin and beards. However intense, how responsible we had to be for our own actions the body had to shut down all but the required techno-knee jerk reactions. We had to mediate the fear as is ran across our mind. We had to meditate to control this hectic river.

Each bend in the river did nothing but hide the shear power of the water. Further rapids double backed in a succession of large reversals. So far the river was at the top end of the limit of navigation, a class 5+. Where 6 is death and 0 is flat. Only a handful of paddlers around the world wish to paddle on water like this. Deep in the Himalayas, even if we didn't want to, we would have to, we had no escape.

Still water lapped on the hull of my boat. The rapids were still intense but in the slack water the pools of tranquil peace below we all collected our thoughts. The hours were pushing on. Downstream the bonding gorge walls fragmented slightly we could see the sun beginning to lower in the sky. What had once been our demon of heat now left behind a haunting chill in its wake. Compressed on the right hand bank was the debris of the GLOF. Squashed and shattered the rock beach was born, as the glacial lake set free with the burst of gallons upon gallons of water. The once destruction now offered sanctity. We would spend the night between the rocks.

The once precise packing of the small dry bags into the back of our kayaks was of little significance. I knew that my bedroom was on the left side of my boat. The blue bag held my thin sleeping back and its waterproof outer. The right side of my boat was full of three different sized bags and I could not remember which one held the spare clothes or the basic food rations or the water purifying kit of iodine. It mattered little since I would need them all at some point. I could take my wet clothes off and walk around naked until my skin dried. Only Martyn and Dave could see. It would be no different than being in a locker room getting changed after a gym session. In such remote surroundings no one would complain if I scattered the contents of my bags across the beach until I found what I needed. No one was likely to visit our camp in the night and remove the items left unpacked until morning. We were alone, with the moon and the small torches our only source of light. The contents of a small packet of dried food was our only fuel.

We had planned for this, we knew that cooked food would be available for most of the river and were willing to take a chance on living on basic foodstuff and sleeping on the beach a few nights. It was part of the expedition; we wanted to be fast and agile on the river. To carry a stove and tent would have weighed the boats down too much. Performance would have been neglected for comfort. It simply wasn't a risk worth taking. The boat needed to do the job correctly. We could paddle when tired and hungry if we understood how the boats would act.

Although not as fulfilling as the hot rice and tea that we had had during the early stages the meal was wanted. To warm ourselves we huddled into our sleeping bags next to a small fire. Hung on sticks and rocks our wet clothes struggled to dry. The heavy dew would soon make then damp again but I was too tired to care. They would get wet soon after we put back on the river anyhow. It was too easy to just curl up in the sleeping bag and drift off to sleep. With the river flowing only feet away and the clear night sky above.

Dave had just put out his last fag of the night whilst Martyn was tucked deep into his waterproof sleeping bag outer. The dim glow of his torch pierced through the fabric and silhouetted a pen in his hand, his diary, his only solace in his environment. I though in scattered daydreams, of the cause and effect of the trip how I wanted to finish the river yet I also wanted it to carry on. Enclosed away from it all as a small collective we knew nothing apart from our own internal politics. The outside world held little significance. The whole world could be at war and we would not now. Maybe it was? Between the snoring and the sound of the river sleep was hard to conquer. I lay staring blankly into the night just waiting for sleep to come.

Once off to sleep I only woke when I heard Dave cough and croak. A smokers cough, regular as clockwork every morning. How relaxing that the noises of the throat can be a human alarm clock? We surfaced slowly, waiting for the sun to break over the surrounding peaks. In the warmth that it would give packing the kayaks again would be a pleasure. It would be a sunny warm start to the day. We lay in our dew-encased sleeping bags chatting about what had been accomplished.

"I reckon that we are almost on the Sun Kosi."

"Yeah me too Daz, what do you think Martyn."

"Could be…dunno."

"If we are then its all easy now, I remember Tom say that it eased of for a day near the confluence."

It took about an hour for the sun to become high in the sky and one again we set off in our boats. Tom was right, his memory had not failed him. Neither had mine. It was back in the 20th century, before the millennium and all the hype, I think, that he along with Craig and Darryl had tackled the Dudh. I was pleased how I had remembered. The river although at times still violent had numerous flat sections. In these places we could chat and take in the surroundings.

Hanging high on the banks were a few villages, some at times were on the riverbanks. Rough fish traps littered the shingle shores whilst dug out wooden fishing boats were often dragged up onto the beaches.

With the population now coming close to the river we knew that it would soon be over. The trail crossed the Sun Kosi and set off slowly up the Dudh Kosi but it faded and was unpopulated for the most part. One days walk from the Sun Kosi was about as far as the houses went. Looking on we estimated that the same would be true for our aquatic descent. On the plus side it meant that we could spend the night in one of the houses and eat hot food again, the welcome would be gracious. Our bellies would be filled and we could save the spare bags of nuts and fruit for our descent down the Sun Kosi. They would have seen few 'white adventurers' on the river and it would be a pleasure to sit in company again with a hot cup of tea.

17
Good Bye My Darling

Will it be remembered in heaven, the joy and dilemma when I pass from this mortal platform? Will the heart and the soul recount the journey as the mind dies? Will the ageing grey hair of retirement enjoy talking of the trip?

No longer does the river hold unknown secrets. No longer does my heart beat with anticipation. The confluence of the Sun Kosi is a welcome sight. Turquoise blue water of the young Dudh Kosi now diluted by the minor tributaries is no longer foaming. Swirling softly, it permeates with a salubrious anthropomorphic mimic as it merges. After all the pulsing froth, where as kayakers running on adrenaline and using our skills to the fullest we were the offspring of the flotsam, the water blends to the warmer water of the major Himalayan drainage the Sun Kosi. Nature has provided a finish line. It was quick and simple. No fan fare. No pot of gold at the end of the rainbow.

Classed as one of the best multi-day trips anywhere in Nepal if not the world was finish enough as it flowed ever onwards

Since breakfast we have been awaiting this moment. Waved off by the villagers whose hospitality had been unsurpassed. The curried eggs and rice had been a fitting last meal on the river. Evident relief on our faces as our teeth tried to push forward through the long growing beards forcing out a smile. Hope sparkled in our eyes and a relaxed dialogue flowed like the river. In the heat of the morning I had put my waterproof dry top in the back of my boat. Sandwiched under my camera and next to my bag of rescue rope it offered a comfortable backrest if nothing else. I only wore a pair of shorts that were well past new and a smelly thermal top. I no longer wore my T-shirt as I feared that all the dirt and debris was forming its own eco-system. When worn on such a hot day I could feel that the red rash of prickly heat would run down my spine. The thermal was just more comfortable. With the relaxed attire I was pleased that the river held no major rapids, no surprises.

A few quick strokes and the kayak, that had been my beast of burden, turned towards the bank just before the river of Everest ended its path. Grounding my boat on the rocky shore was a relief. I jump out of the seat. I knew that this journey is not the true finish of the trip but the Dudh Kosi mingled with the drainage of the Sun Kosi on its way to India.

All paddle strokes will now be on the Sun Kosi. Stretching my arms skyward reaching for the heavens my neck is involuntary thrown back in ecstasy. As my spine cracks I feel the tension escape. I want to remember this moment since the river has taken so much, as much if not more than I wanted to give. All the past emotions and the pathological visions of social outcast were washed way. I felt content and cleansed. I had fulfilled my obligation to the river and to myself but I had hurt many on the way without just cause. I felt the river now owed me. It had driven me for months and seeing the river at the end of a tunnel I had rushed headlong. Not concerned with anything else in my life. Now it would be time to face the past.

"What can you give me?" My inner voice asked of the immortal tendencies of the spirit if they exist at all, how have you allowed this expedition? The river had been my whole world both Heaven and Hell, God and the Devil, Allah and Ganesh, Buddha and Jehovah. It meant everything to me yet it was inconsequential to people I would pass in the street.

It would be doubtful that the river would ever miss a small pebble from just under the water line. My tired and heavy right arm could only grasp a small gem of rock, cracked and imperfect. Running my fingers over the rugged chips and creases it is drawn close to my eye line.

"Thanks, it's ideal." I whisper to the wind whilst drawing the rock to my lips before putting it in my pocket. Getting back in my boat I loosen the backrest and place my helmet between my legs. Floating I continue down the Sun Kosi to join my friends.

A humid wind blows softy up from the flat land of India just beyond the town of Chatra. As the hills that have been so claustrophobic during the journey slowly fade away. All that has gone before is behind us and stretching out in front is the frontier, the open gate letting us out of the river. The gate can only be opened through a passage down the river, through all that is behind and all that has been accomplished. The significance of what my body has gone through. Succinctly the bijou emotions, that I find difficult to express, fade just as the surroundings, mellow. It is just another day on the river. Even though I try to piece together the scribbling from my diary I cannot explain what I feel.

Floating alone on the river, even though friends are all around. We have all got our demons to fight and the truth of such cannot simply be washed away by the water. It must also be washed away from inside. Simply I wished my parents were able to see what I had done, to see where I was. I hope that for some strange reason my Brother, Mother, Father and all my Grandparents are having a family day out and stroll on the confluence beaches.

Looking to the beach my Aged Grandfather, Fred, stood with his walking stick and flat cap laid juxtaposed to his simple honest smile. I so wanted to shake his hand and say so many things that I had never said before. But you never tell people when they are alive how much they mean to you. Until I felt empty from the river journey I never knew what had been given to me, where I had got the energy and how it came to this.

"Thank you for giving me solid foundations but also helping me build wings so that I can fly." I turned to the beach and spoke softly in cliché to my family. Peering over his stick, like some Hobbitesque legend, my Granddad the obscure guru nodded.

"Arr, very good lad, very good," then his image faded into the sand as he saluted solemnly with his arthritic hand. A hand weak in appearance and stained with the years of hard work of almost a century in use.

Tears sit uncomfortably in my eyes as the energy and adrenaline seep away. With the loss of energy I want to distance myself from what has led me to this. I just hope that the whole experience can help me develop as a person. I hope that I can cope with the consequences of my actions. Memories are just ghostly spirits that pass as illusions in the night. All is now placid and I am drained. A mind that was once filled with thoughts and plans now vacuous, as questions flowed into its empty space. So much had been given to get to this point. Goal and aims needed to be re-evaluated.

I wonder should we have done this river? Why not, isn't life just an adventure and the time we spend just a gathering of experiences? Primary learning at its best but no one really cares for such selfishness in today's modern world do they?

Idols fail the populace, falling to the sirens cause destruction yet we are pulled towards oblivion, towards finding truth. If I though I knew nothing then that would be something. Alas I think I know something and that is not everything. That is not the truth to behold.

Epilogue

The final days on the river were spent with a commercial raft company who we bumped into. We knew the guides well and they fed us whilst also arranging our transport back to the office in Kathmandu.

Since finishing the trip Martyn did indeed settle down to domestic life whilst Dave and myself returned to Asia in 2004 to kayak the rivers of Pakistan and the Braldu river that flows from K2. As small time expedition river runners I wondered if we would be pleased and content by the security of a firm job, mortgage and keeping up with the neighbours.

Without the help of friends the expedition would have been unthinkable. It would be thankless to credit everyone but special thanks must go to the following, the rest know who you are. Thanks go to all those that have coached us in our formative years and our close friends at Drift and Trek Nepal. Ultimate Rivers for the food and bus ride away from the Sun Kosi. Also thanks to Perception Kayaks, System X, Nookie, Vagabond, Robson, Tim Thomas, Artistic, Tradewinds, Corvedale Care and the Upstairs Jazz Bar in Kathmandu.

Other Travel Books Available From Urban Fox Press

'The Seeker'
By David Wise
£7.00
An extraordinary journey through the deserts, mountains and religions of the Middle East in search of Love, Faith and the Cult of the Moon.

'Scatterlings'
By David Wise
£8.00
Collected Travel Prose and Photography 1990 – 2003

'In Egypt'
By David Wise
£6.00
Another Egyptian walk, this time a week long odyssey south from Luxor in the company of religious zealots, sandstorms and always, always, the meandering River Nile...

To purchase any of these books please fill in the order form opposite, make your cheques payable to 'Urban Fox Press', and send to;
Urban Fox Press, 6 Albert Road, Chatham,
Kent, England, ME4 5PZ, UK.

URBAN FOX PRESS ORDER FORM

Name;...

Address;...

....

Email;...

Please indicate which titles you would like and how many.

Title	Price	Quantity
'The Seeker'	£7.00	
'Scatterlings'	£8.00	
'In Egypt'	£6.00	
Sub Total	£	
P&P UK £1.75 per book	£	
P&P Worldwide £3.75 per book	£	
Total	£	